TWAYNE'S WORLD AUTHORS SERIES

A Survey of the World's Literature

Sylvia E. Bowman, Indiana University

GENERAL EDITOR

LATIN LITERATURE

Professor Philip Levine, University of California

EDITOR

Horace

 73

TWAYNE'S WORLD AUTHORS SERIES (TWAS)

The purpose of TWAS is to survey the major writers —novelists, dramatists, historians, poets, philosophers, and critics—of the nations of the world. Among the national literatures covered are those of Australia, Canada, China, Eastern Europe, France, Germany, Greece, India, Italy, Japan, Latin America, New Zealand, Poland, Russia, Scandinavia, Spain and the African nations, as well as Hebrew, Yiddish, and Latin Classical literatures. This survey is complemented by Twayne's United States Authors Series and English Authors Series.

The intent of each volume in these series is to present a critical-analytical study of the works of the writer; to include biographical and historical material that may be necessary for understanding, appreciation, and critical appraisal of the writer; and to present all material in clear, concise English—but not to vitiate the scholarly content of the work by doing so.

Horace

By KENNETH J. RECKFORD

University of North Carolina

Twayne Publishers, Inc.　: :　New York

101162

Preface

The realization of my long-time intention, to describe Horace's growth as a poet and as a man, has been greatly facilitated by the appearance in the last decade of two books, Eduard Fraenkel's *Horace* and Steele Commager's *The Odes of Horace*. Before these appeared, it was virtually impossible to avoid giving undue importance either to philological *Quellensuchung* or to the so-called new criticism; but today we can see that each makes a valid but limited contribution to our enjoyment and understanding of Horace's poetry—a goal in which scholar and critic (a sometimes unreal distinction) may ultimately concur. Alongside these two forms of investigation, of Horace's relation to his Greek and Roman masters, and the inner structure of his discrete poems, I have tried to establish the importance of a third. What shape and meaning has Horace's poetry taken as a whole? Or, differently: can we trace the development of Horace's imagination and thought through his poetry? There are other poets of whom this quasi-biographical question should not be asked. For Horace, as we shall see, it is fully appropriate.

To meet the requirements set by Twayne Publishers, I was compelled to be highly selective in the poems I discuss; to cut analyses short, taking many interesting points of diction, sound-patterning, rhythm, and literary allusion for granted; to omit almost all of the Latin quotations from the *Satires* and *Epistles*, leaving only the English translations; and to prune footnotes. (The translations, all my own, were compressed proportionately. About eighty per cent literal, for the non-Latinist, they were sometimes altered for amusement.) Yet dieting, though painful, can in the long run prove beneficial; and perhaps a slender volume can creep, like Horace's little fox, into places where thicker ones cannot enter. If a brief, yet balanced and reasonably documented view of Horace and his poetry can supplement the special interests of classical scholars, instruct Latin students, and also convey, without watering it down too much, something of the wine of Horace's poetic wisdom to the wider audience of "knights" in whom he himself was so interested, I shall be quite content.

It is time now to thank Professor Philip Levine for commissioning this book and editing it carefully, and to acknowledge with gratitude some long-standing debts: to Mr. Norman L. Hatch, of the Phillips Exeter Academy, who taught me to read Latin poetry; to teachers at Harvard, Dr. Robert A. Brooks, now Assistant Secretary of the Army, and Professor J. P. Elder, who between them led me to enjoy Horace's satires and odes; to the Fulbright Commission, for a year's study in Rome in 1954-55, and to Professor L. R. Taylor and the American Academy in Rome for their hospitality during that year; to Professor Michael C. J. Putnam, for many enlightening discussions of Latin poetry; and not least, to my colleagues at Chapel Hill, especially Professor Berthe M. Marti, for their unfailing kindness and encouragement.

A still older debt is to my father, Joseph S. Reckford (1904-49). This book is dedicated to his memory.

at hoc nunc
laus illi debetur et a me gratia maior.

KENNETH J. RECKFORD

University of North Carolina,
Chapel Hill

Contents

Chronology

(All dates are B.C.)

70	Virgil born.
65	December 8, Quintus Horatius Flaccus born at Venusia, in Southern Italy.
63	Consulship of Cicero.
59	The First Triumvirate: Caesar, Crassus, Pompey.
55?–45	Horace educated in Rome.
48	Caesar defeats Pompey at Pharsalus.
43	The Second Triumvirate: Antony, Lepidus, Octavian. Horace a military tribune in Brutus' republican army.
42	Antony and Octavian defeat Brutus and Cassius at Philippi.
42–41	Horace returns to Rome, begins *Epodes* and *Satires*.
39–38	Publication of Virgil's *Eclogues*. Horace introduced to Maecenas.
35–34	Publication of *Satires, Book I.*
31	September 2, Octavian defeats Antony (and Cleopatra) at Actium.
31–30	Publication of *Satires, Book II,* and *Epodes.*
30–29	Publication of Virgil's *Georgics.* The *Aeneid* begun.

27   Octavian "restores the Republic to the Senate and Roman people," lays down unconstitutional powers, and receives the name Augustus. Probable completion of Horace's "Roman Odes."

24–
23   Publication of *Odes* I-III.

23–
18   Horace's "retirement."

20   Publication of *Epistles* I.

19   Death of Virgil. The *Aeneid* published posthumously.

19–
18   *Epistles,* II, 2. Most probable date also of *Epistles,* II, 3. (the *Ars Poetica*).

17   June 1-3, the Secular Games. *Carmen Saeculare.*

13   Publication of *Odes* IV. Consecration of the Altar of Peace (dedicated in 9).

13–
12   *Epistles* II, 1.

8   Death of Maecenas; and, a few months later, November 27, death of Horace.

CHAPTER 1

The Rose and the Vine[1]

I *Deceptive Simplicity*

IT is certain that Horace cannot instruct or be known except through his poetry. Remove his precepts, like *carpe diem* or *aurea mediocritas,* from their living contexts, and they wither like branches cut from trees: that is the alpha and omega of modern Horatian criticism. Yet it is also certain that the Satires, Odes, or Epistles themselves disintegrate in the withering light of critical analysis if we isolate them too long from the human experience which informs them and the larger, growing organism, whose unfolding and maturation they embody when taken altogether. Horace's life is itself a work of art; it pleases us by its architectonic completeness; and it contributes to our own education and growth, to the degree, perhaps, that we realize with what pain it was achieved; for, in Horace's words, the poet resembles the ballet dancer who "will look like one who plays, and will suffer agony":

ludentis speciem dabit et torquebitur.[2]

Perfection of art and sanity of outlook are hard won, but they are—or so Horace helps convince us—worth the cost.

Although, therefore, we shall begin by analyzing a single ode, I, 38, we shall not stop there; for Horace's personality and growth are best seen, not in flashes of detail or in the architecture of single poems, but in the light one poem sheds on another, the steady light cast by the imaginative interconnectedness and totality of a life's work.

Here is the ode.

> Persicos odi, puer, apparatus,
> displicent nexae philyra coronae;
> mitte sectari, rosa quo locorum
>   sera moretur.

simplici myrto nihil allabores
sedulus curo: neque te ministrum
dedecet myrtus neque me sub arta
   vite bibentem.

(Don't bring me Persian trappings, boy;
 garlands of lindenbark displease me;
 don't seek out wherever on earth the
 late rose lingers. Don't trouble to add
 anything to the plain myrtle: that becomes
 you, the servant, and me too, drinking
 beneath the close-joined trellis.)

Meaning as well as beauty perishes in translation, or in paraphrase. Evidently, Horace renounces the luxurious elaboration
of life symbolized in stanza 1 and chooses simplicity and restraint
in stanza 2: a sensible antithesis—but is it emotionally convincing?
Or why (to be personal) should I, after reading this ode, be any
more content with teaching in a small Southern town? Why yearn
any the less for escargots à la Bourguignonne (we have no French
restaurant), or Nilsson at the Met, or a handful, just a small handful, of Manets and Gauguins, Renoirs and Van Goghs?

But the poem is more than the paraphrase, and it does carry
conviction. In a dramatic sequence of feeling and thought Horace
faces the temptation we face daily, of what Samuel Johnson called
"novelty,"[3] and overcomes it, but not without a struggle. The dis-
missal of luxury in line 1 is deceptively easy. *Persicos* suggests
Eastern decadence, and *apparatus*, empty, rattling bombast. Nobody wants that. Line 2, though, with its pleasing liquid sounds
and images (the Greek word *philyra* may be resolved into "love"
and "lyre"; Philyra, mother of the wise centaur Chiron, was transformed into the linden tree: so will Horace renounce love, music,
metamorphosis?), prepares us for the lovely garland of words,

sectari, rosa quo locorum
   sera moretur.

The sensuous image lingers in our minds, evoking thoughts of
transient beauty and autumnal pathos, the romance of travel and
pursuit, the lure of the unattainable.

Does the *rosa sera* "run away with the poem"? That would be romantic. Follow Horace: his myrtle is more than it seems. Its attribute, *simplici,* echoes *displicent* in sound and *nexae* in idea; it means more than "plain": something more like "woven into unity." The myrtle receives its own elaborate sound pattern. The vine-trellis is "interwoven." This is no ordinary simplicity: the poet's eye has rediscovered what is most special in what seemed most ordinary and familiar.[4]

Odes I, 38 is unified by the image of weaving and the ideas it symbolizes, of art and the harmonious life. Weaving is an ancient metaphor for the making of poetry. Pindar wove "garlands of song" for his victors; so Horace, for a friend. But while in Odes I, 38 "weaving" suggests poetic artistry—the interlacing of words, here exemplified, in a complex pattern of sound and meaning (what Nietzsche praised as Horace's "mosaic work") —it also embodies his choice of life, which is deceptively simple. The lesson is at once esthetic and moral. Less is more, as an architect recently decreed.[5] Elsewhere, Horace describes a flirtatious girl as *simplex munditiis*: plain and neat, with much underlying artifice.[6] His lyrics are like that. So is his life.

Already, then, we see why Horace's philosophy cannot be abstracted without harm from the poetry embodying it. As Commager has said: "Only by yielding ourselves fully to the demands of Horace's verse, and thus to the enjoyment it conveys, can his poems say something that is significantly true rather than obviously true."[7] Odes I, 38 teaches us as it moves and pleases us. The completion of the thought coincides with that of the poem: Horace, like most good poets,[8] resembles the little girl who asked her impatient mother, "How can I know what I mean till I see what I say?" But the ode is didactic as well as meditative; for although Horace intends no immediate practical effect on a definite audience (the *puer* is a dramatic device), he knows that we shall eavesdrop. As Richard Reitzenstein said in 1924: "Liberation of yourself and influence on others almost always go together, consciously or unconsciously."[9] Friedrich Klingner, that most humane scholar, was equally right in reversing the proposition in 1929: "Horace's poetry is an instrument not only of instruction and guidance, but even more, of self-formation."[10] How the two are "interwoven" in a new harmony, at once Hellenistic and classical, will be explored in later chapters.

[13]

II *Variety and Contrast*

The resolution of Odes I, 38 is temporary, a moment of achieved calm. Who knows what new onslaught of anxiety or discontent may occupy Horace as he drinks beneath that vine-trellis? His life can assume other colors, other shapes.

Odes I, 38 was studied in isolation; it is also, significantly, third in a group of drinking poems. How different the first is! In Odes I, 36, a friend's dear friend has returned safe from Spain. Horace greets the occasion, not with the full emotional involvement of a Catullus, but with the sympathetic awareness that moderation and restraint—the usual Horatian lessons—are sometimes out of place; let joy be unconfined:

> neu promptae modus amphorae,
> neu morem in Salium sit requies pedum,
>   neu multi Damalis meri
> Bassum Threicia vincat amystide,
>   neu desint epulis rosae
> neu vivax apium neu breve lilium.
>   omnes in Damalin putres
> deponent oculos, nec Damalis novo
>   divelletur adultero,
> lascivis hederis ambitiosior.

> (Let the wine-cup pass without limit, let feet
> keep to the Salian beat without rest; let Damalis,
> distinguished in drinking, not surpass Bassus in
> chug-a-lugging wine; don't let roses give out, or
> water-parsley that stays green, or the short-lived
> lily. All will gaze on Damalis with melting eyes,
> nor will Damalis be torn away from a new paramour:
> Damalis, more all-embracing than the wanton ivy.)

Wildness will be right. Meter and internal rhyme suggest stamping of feet. Rational limit, *modus*, is rejected. The rose reappears, in winter more luxurious than ever;[11] and *breve lilium* makes the point clear: life is short, embrace its brief joys. So Damalis ("Frisky") will embrace her man, clinging like ivy (contrast the tranquil "entwining" in Odes I, 38). The image, of sportive sexuality, perfectly embodies the poem's unphilosophical mood.

In Odes I, 37, Horace passes from an initial call to drink, for Cleopatra is dead (a first line borrowed directly from the sixth-century Greek poet Alcaeus, who was celebrating a tyrant's death), to memories of the once dreaded queen: her drunken hopes of empire, her sobering defeat, the final "draught" of the asp's venom by which will triumphed over weakness: she would never walk in Octavian's triumph! Horace's own thoughts turn sober like Cleopatra's mind as the fumes of intoxication are dispelled. The ending, as in I, 38, is quiet and serious. Yet Cleopatra, as Commager observes, has something of the late rose about her,[12] and Horace lets his heart go out to her, as Virgil's does to Dido in Aeneid IV. The open, even romantic, ending provides a strong contrast with the following ode.

Nor is Odes I, 36-38 the only constellation to which I, 38 belongs and by which its meaning is enlarged. Odes I, 1, the other framing poem of Book I, also deals with Horace's choice of life. It too begins with renunciation. Horace (the form is traditional) will not associate himself with "those who" seek athletic victories (dusty), political honors (empty), excessive wealth (why bother?). More to his taste are quieter lives, of the small farmer or gentleman:

> est qui nec veteris pocula Massici
> nec partem solido demere de die
> spernit, nunc viridi membra sub arbuto
> stratus, nunc ad aquae lene caput sacrae.

> (One man there is who spurns not cups of old
> Massic or to subtract part of the day's store:
> he stretches his limbs beneath the green
> arbutus, or lies by the gentle source of a
> holy spring.)

Is this Horace? The conceit of "breaking off" a piece of time to accompany your drink is Horatian; the well-placed adjectives too, emphasizing the freshness, even sacredness of relaxation. But after two further lives, of the warrior and hunter, are satirically described, a more adequate representation of Horace's choice of life emerges:

me doctarum hederae praemia frontium
dis miscent superis, me gelidum nemus
nympharumque leves cum Satyris chori
secernunt populo, si neque tibias
Euterpe cohibet nec Polyhymnia
Lesboum refugit tendere barbiton.
quodsi me lyricis vatibus inseres,
sublimi feriam sidera vertice.

(The ivy crown, meed of learned foreheads,
joins me with the gods above; the cold grove,
the light-dancing Nymphs and Satyrs, set me
apart from the throng—let only Euterpe not
withhold the flute or Polyhymnia the Lesbian
lyre. If you place me among the inspired bards,
I'll rise to strike the heavens with my brow.)

Horace is a poet first and last. Although he, like the *est qui*, enjoys leisure, seclusion, and companionship with nature, this is only
one side of life; the poet also achieves success like the athlete or
general. His pride of achievement is partly shown, as in Odes
III, 30 (the other framing ode of the *collection*), by metaphors of
rising and climbing and by the Asclepiadic meter, which is almost
processional. How different is the modest

neque me, sub arta
vite bibentem.

Such contrasts, practically speaking, are infinite. A "field of
force" exists, not just, as Nietzsche perceived, in the separate
strophe or ode, but in the collection. Apparently, Horace arranged
the 88 odes of Books I-III to display the variety of his moods, not
just his meters. Light and serious, political and convivial poems
are amusingly, often very suggestively, juxtaposed like Shakespeare's scenes. In adjoining poems, like I, 36-38, a common theme
may receive different treatment, or diverse subject matter conceal
similarity of feeling. In spite of its formal and tonal complexity
the collection of Odes has, however, a certain unity: not the organic unity (*simplex et unum*) of the single ode,[13] or the *Aeneid;*
but an implied, subjective unity, partly evident in the way one

poem sheds light on another (as I, 1 on I, 38, and vice versa); partly, too, in our growing intuition of the personality of Horace, in the world of whose imagination we are learning to move with the assurance bred of familiarity, and whose figure—playful, ironic, elusive, yet *simplex munditiis*—we are surely beginning to discern.

III *Continuity of Growth*

Let us look further. Although Horace's diverse publications span most of his thinking life (see the chronology), and although we, like his contemporaries, have our preferences, "some liking odes, other iambs, others black-salted satire";[14] despite, too, Horace's own frequently misleading assertions of different levels of intent, we can still trace through Satires, Odes, and Epistles the continuity of a mind that reflects, and with increasing penetration, on the same matters of the human heart.

Thus we may turn from Odes I, 38 to Satires II, 6, written perhaps seven years before. The satire describes Horace's contentment with his present situation. His Sabine farm, a recent gift from Maecenas, is all he wants; Mercury, god of luck, need provide nothing more. Satire proper enters in when Horace contrasts his rural happiness with the irritation of urban "busy-ness" (*negotium*: literally, "denial of leisure"). Personal commissions, committee work, social obligations: these are necessary things; indeed, many of them are derived from Horace's relationship to Maecenas, in which he takes pride; but cumulatively they ruin good days. After this negative picture, Horace portrays his untroubled *otium* in the country: the sleep, the hours of daytime laziness, time to read the classics (Greek, of course), and good philosophical talks with friends about things that matter, like virtue, ethical choice, and friendship, not the sophisticated gossip of Society. In illustrating right conversation, Horace shifts back indirectly to the city. Cervius, a shrewd farmer, tells the fable of the Country Mouse and the City Mouse. This is the heart of the satire.

The City Mouse pays a visit. With some effort and embarrassment, his friend attempts to entertain him comfortably; "finally" (a hint of bursting impatience), the visitor launches his attack (lines 90-97):

tandem urbanus ad hunc "quid te iuvat" inquit, "amice,
praerupti nemoris patientem vivere dorso?
vis tu homines urbemque feris praeponere silvis?
carpe viam, mihi crede, comes; terrestria quando
mortalis animas vivunt sortita, neque ulla est
aut magno aut parvo leti fuga: quo, bone, circa,
dum licet, in rebus iucundis vive beatus;
vive memor, quam sis aevi brevis."

(Finally the city dweller speaks up. "How can you
live, my friend, above these rugged woods? It's
a wild place—choose a human life, in the city!
Take to the road with me; you can trust me;
for earthborn creatures are endowed with
perishable souls, and there's no escaping
death for great or small; so, while you may,
live it up in bliss and comfort! Always keep
in mind how little life you have.")

The appeal has been called Epicurean, but that is misleading.
The injunction, "Eat, drink, and be merry," perverts Epicurus'
refined, even ascetic teachings about time and pleasure. No more
genuine philosophy dwells in this urbane Mouse than in Petro-
nius' *bourgeois gentilhomme*, Trimalchio, who encourages his
guests to drink up by having a skeleton dandled on the table. For
all its vulgarity, though, the temptation is serious. There is the
glitter of the metropolis, its sophistication, its intensity of life
(suggested by the Socratic contrast of men with trees). More important is the urge to grasp eagerly at life because it is short, to
clutch its riches in our hands, to sell our spiritual freedom for
pottage—what the mob calls "bliss." The Country Mouse quite
succumbs. He tries the city, finds it far from bliss, and runs back
(the dogs are barking) to the safety and goodness of his earlier
life. The inner drama, if city and country are taken to symbolize
states of mind, comes very close to that of Odes I, 38: the initial
rejection of luxury and excess, the emotional flirtation with the
rosa sera, and the return to a simple life subtly enriched in the
process.

A passage from Epistles I, 8, written a few years after the ode,
shows Horace in a very different mood. He is living, he complains,

"neither rightly nor pleasantly," not from material losses, but because (lines 7-12):

> . . . mente minus validus quam corpore toto
> nil audire velim, nil discere, quod levet aegrum;
> fidis offendar medicis, irascar amicis,
> cur me funesto properent arcere veterno;
> quae nocuere sequar, fugiam quae profore credam;
> Romae Tibur amem ventosus, Tibure Romam.

> (. . . I'm unwell, in mind more than physique; can't
> stand to hear or learn what might relieve me,
> resent trusted doctors, get cross at friends
> for warding off death-bringing lethargy;
> pursue known harm, run from expected help; at
> Rome, want Tibur, and at Tibur, Rome.)

The polarities are familiar: consider Satires II, 6, or else II, 7,
where Davus, the slave, preaching on holiday, cites Horace's wav-
ering between city and country as a symptom of irresolution and
inconsistency. What is new in the epistle is the undertone of despair. The more deeply you realize that "All is vanity," the more
vigorously the demon of *acedia*, not caring, will occupy the house
vacated by lesser demons of avarice, ambition, or luxury. Perhaps
this is gerrymandering: the tone of Epistles I, 8 is not typical of
that collection, although the theme of sickness and health abounds
there. The point is that the City Mouse and the *rosa sera* were
never rejected once and for all. Horace attacked inconsistency and
inordinate desire from his first satire to his last epistle. Old symbols, like city and country, renew and extend themselves as he
continues to ask the same few questions, but with deepening insight: what is the good life, and how can Man attain it?

Comparison of these and other passages, then, while enhancing
their meaning, shows from what a continuity and depth of personal experience and thought his light-dancing precepts arise. Might
we go further and say that rightness of growth is the chief lesson
Horace teaches? That he followed Pindar's cryptic advice, *genoio
hoios essi mathôn* ("Learn what you are, and that become"), is
shown in many ways: in the progressive certainty with which he
formulated literary aims and established a right relation to earlier

masters; in the tenacious search by which he made clear to himself what the state meant to him, and he to the state; and in the expansion of his philosophy of life, not, as is often thought, in the direction of a careless scepticism, but rather towards an increasingly painful openness to the reality of things, upon which a poem can only bestow impermanent unity and meaning. We cannot stress enough Horace's imaginative ability to weave these diverse strands of experience, literary, social, political, and philosophical, into an integral and complete pattern of art and life. At the same time, we must admire his power to endure experience, not just through humor, the ironic smile that could be a defense against pain, but also through a courage of mind that has, it seems, never sufficiently been praised.

CHAPTER 2

The Transformation of Satire [1]

I Anger and Detachment

THE realm of satire, as it is generally conceived, belongs to the fiercest, to Juvenal, Swift, and Goya, who despise contemporary society and hate the "damned human race." To them, man is a vicious, sinful creature, as far beneath the horse or donkey as, through his rational faculty, he should be above them. Such satirists may regard themselves as surgeons who with their pen, as with knife or cautery, will attempt a final operation on the corrupt body of society, or else, hoping for no cure, they may still write from what Juvenal called *indignatio*, a burning sense of the unfairness of things that must find an outlet. Their laughter is scornful and desperate, furious in proportion to its hopelessness. Theirs is the "tragic buskin," the grand style, the rhetorical invective of a hell-fire and damnation preacher.

There exists, however, another satirical species which Horace fathered and to which Erasmus, Pope (in his better moments), and Dr. Johnson belong. On the assumption that man is capable of rational conduct, they attempt to improve society by placing men's faults in a true perspective. Rather than denounce our crimes, they encourage us tactfully to overcome our weaknesses. Their flexible, humorous language, their unobtrusive, usually ironic conversational style conform to that intention. Thus Persius, whose own satire heralded Juvenal's, contrasted Horace with his more vehement forerunner, Lucilius (*c.* 180-102 B.C.):

> Lucilius lashed the city, you Lupus, and you, Mucius,
> and broke his jawbone on them; sly Flaccus makes his
> friend laugh and tickles his every fault, playing
> around his heartstrings, unsnots his nose and
> shrewdly snubs the people: mayn't I mutter a word?[2]

Notice how Horace's pose is defined for posterity. He is an ironist, indulges in the superiority of saying less than he means, and operates on our characters under the guise of a dinner companion. In the eighteenth century, he will write for the morning *Spectator* or *Rambler*; in the twentieth, he will be a free-lance critic, reviewer of books, and occasional lecturer on college campuses. The pose is much the same.

Which type of satire a man writes will be influenced by his literary antecedents and milieu, his social and political environment, the *Zeitgeist,* and his own temperament, imagination, and sense of direction (if he has one). Simplifications are always tempting. Thus the handbooks of Latin literature inform us that Horace was sociable by disposition; that Persius returned to rougher, more primitive satire because the Neronian Age was decadent; that Juvenal wrote from resentment of his poverty and unrequited merit. All this is conjecture. Surely it would be preferable to avoid biography, to concentrate more impersonally on stylistic matters, on the *persona* used by the satirist, and his place in an identifiable rhetorical tradition?

Let us by all means distrust simplifications, including Horace's own. His *apologia* in Satires I, 4, that he "jots down notes" to improve his character, is disingenuous. His explanation in Satires I, 10, that he selected satire as a free field, pre-empted by no able contemporary and suitable, as a minor genre, to his talents, is ex post facto and incomplete. And he evidently does not write, as he professes in Satires II, 1, simply in self-defense—or because he cannot sleep.

Scepticism is unavoidable. Nobody wants to be taken in. Yet conjecture can be valuable in literary studies, as in historical: we must sometimes ask, not just what happened, but what might have happened, if we hope to understand the past, not just explain it. Why did Horace follow a different path from Lucilius? Why didn't he write like Juvenal? If his ironic and retroactive explanations are inadequate and misleading, and his satires were not a planned unity, can they be understood in process of development? Perhaps we can read between Horace's lines, can catch glimpses of changes in his attitudes toward life and society which are reflected in his gradual redefinition of his satiric place, purpose, and style. If this approach, which accords with our central theme, of right growth, still errs on the side of biographical conjecture, not to say teleology, this is perhaps a healthy reaction to the depersonalized criticism, itself a reaction against vague impressionism, that has become fashionable in our century.

In a late, autobiographical passage in Epistles II, 2, Horace says that "bold poverty impelled" him to write (lines 41-54):

> It happened, I was brought up at Rome, where
> I learned how Achilles' wrath damaged the Greeks.
> Good Athens furthered my ability: I tried to dis-
> tinguish straight from crooked, and seek the truth
> among the groves of Academe. Hard times dislodged
> me from that pleasant spot. The surge of civil
> war swept me, untrained, to arms—not matching
> Caesar Augustus' muscles. And when Philippi
> let me go, low-down, my wings clipped, without a
> father's shelter or estate, bold poverty impelled
> me to write verses. Now, with unfailing plenty,
> how could I ever be brainwashed enough to write
> more verses when I could be sleeping?

Horace's "poverty" is probably a red herring. The point lies rather in his "boldness" of attitude.[3] We should recall the anecdote told just previously, of the soldier of Lucullus whose wallet was stolen: "a raging wolf, then, wrathful at himself and the foe alike, with starving teeth, he boldly stormed a royal citadel" (lines 28-30). The overt parallel between the soldier and Horace is that both "fought" when necessary and rested when possible. But *iratus* makes another connection. The soldier fought, not just from need, but from anger at his material loss; Horace wrote with Achilles-like wrath (the satirist is often compared to a wolf) because of the failure of personal ambitions and political hopes. It is easy to draw the picture of "Horace in Grub Street": uprooted by the war, a displaced person after Philippi, his father dead, his inheritance confiscated, he himself compelled to accept boredom and drudgery as a *scriba quaestorius*, or minor civil servant. The question is, do his writings display the frustrated resentment we would expect in a man whose wings were prematurely clipped?

Certain epodes may. In particular, Epode 4, a lampoon on an ex-slave who fought his way to riches, ostentation, and a military tribunate, suggests both personal bitterness and, considering Horace's situation, a certain impropriety. Yet even here, and more successfully in other, perhaps later epodes, the poet's anger—however real its causes—has been transmuted into humor and art.

In the epodes, Horace said later, he adopted the "measures and spirit" of the seventh-century poet Archilochus, "not his content, nor the words hounding Lycambes to death."[4] The statement is partially misleading. Archilochus was *audax*, a free-lance soldier and writer who killed, or intended to kill, with words as with the spear, a great hater: in short, the archetypal satirist. But Horace adopts his spirit playfully. He is a self-conscious artist, as Archilochus was not; and he writes with an eye to self-conscious Hellenistic poets, notably Callimachus, who saw in the iambs and choliambs of Archilochus and Hipponax an untrammeled art form susceptible of refinement and delicate irony. The Roman Neoterics or "moderns" of the generation before Horace admired Callimachus and adhered to his critical precepts. They must have considered iambs or choliambs a suitable, since minor, form for the novice to experiment with. One such collection, entitled *Catalepta*, "Poems in the Subtle Vein," is attributed to young Virgil— "elements," says an epigram, "of the divine poet, his untrained Muse in various strains of song."[5] Doubtless, Horace's epodes also began as apprentice work. We must not read too much personal or moral content into them. The obscene epodes 8 and 12 are a play form,[6] not expressions of moral indignation at the lewd old women there depicted. Yet however much Horace refined the iambic form with Hellenistic wit, he may still have been attracted to Archilochus personally as the poet whom "rage armed with the iamb, its proper weapon."[7] Hatred can be transformed. But we may suspect, as we read these early poems, that hatred once was there.

In his earliest satires, Horace wears the mask of the Cynic preacher who, himself not passion's slave, scorns the mass of humankind as fools and triflers. The ethical standards here implied are derived from Greek popular philosophy and are Horatian enough: sense, moderation, independence, living according to nature. In style, intention, and spirit, however, Satires I, 2 and I, 1 should be distinguished from Horace's riper *sermones,* or "conversations." His shifting relation to Lucilius complicates the point.

Horace was first attracted to what seemed a Roman adaptation of the Greek "diatribe." To look on mortal folly with the indifference of a Bion of Borysthenes (a third-century homilist) offered comfort after failure. Ironically, though, as will be shown, Horace's satire became more Lucilian in spirit after he abandoned the diatribe form, became technically independent, and gave back to satire its right tone and function, of personal and Roman expression.

A long road leads from Satires I, 2 to II, 6. The contrast is impressive. If the earlier satire has a bitter olive's pungency, it fails as art from indecisiveness. It lacks purpose, and it lacks personality.

After a preamble about men's contradictory pursuits (as, now hoarding, now squandering money), the preacher of Satires I, 2 rebukes extremism in sexual matters. Adultery and passion are silly. Satisfaction without emotional involvement is recommended; prostitutes will serve best. The satire holds together, partly through the concept of right limit, for sex is treated here much as money is treated in Satires I, 1 (although the praises of prostitution square badly with the speaker's earlier emphasis on the Mean, and Aristotelian, Epicurean, and Cynic commonplaces make strange bedfellows); but still more, through a consistently impersonal and cynical tone, still audible today in a saying highly regarded by sophomores: "Why buy a cow, when milk is so cheap?"

Not Horace's obscenity, but its lack is here in question: or better, his vacillation between two satiric-comic ideals. Satires I, 2 attacks individuals but is not personal enough. At times, Horace seems nostalgic; he wishes he were Aristophanes, or an Aristophanic Lucilius; yet the fools and knaves he attacks by name are mere ghosts, literary shadows. Had Aristophanic comedy been sanctioned at Rome, apart from occasional ritual lampooning, as at military triumphs, and had Horace been able to mount his attacks from the secure position of a Lucilius, a knight and Scipio's friend, he still lacked the gusto for insult and invective. The material was there. It always is. Tigellius, quack and poetaster, would have graced a Dunciad: when does he come to life in Horace's verses? Maecenas was eccentric and effeminate, an obvious butt for the Old Comedy. But Horace indiscriminately lumps together his future patron with a faceless *est qui* (lines 25-26):

> Maltinus tunicis demissis ambulat; est qui
> inguen ad obscenum subductis usque facetus,
> (Maltinus, ambling, trails his tunic, another thinks
> he's clever, tucking it up to his privates . . .)[8]

and with that silly pair, perfumed Rufillus and stinking Gargonius. A comic writer should fish or cut bait. He should lacerate the sinner, like Aristophanes, or typify the sin, like Menander, in carefully and sympathetically sketched characters; caricature broadly like Plautus, or search like Terence for the elusive mean between the ridiculous, inhuman extremes. Horace's satire on the passion of love owes much to Book 4 of Lucretius' *De Rerum Natura;* but if Lucretius, like the satirist, "observes the sea of human folly from reason's safe shore,"[9] Horace lacks, in Satires I, 2, his psychological penetration, his passionate sympathy with passion's slaves, his determination to draw them to Epicurus' shores of light.

A glance at the funniest lines of the satire suggests what went wrong (68-76):

> huic si mutonis verbis mala tanta videnti
> diceret haec animus: "quid vis tibi? numquid ego a te
> magno prognatum deposco consule cunnum
> velatumque stola mea cum conferbuit ira?"
> quid responderet? "magno patre nata puella est."
> at quanto meliora monet pugnantiaque istis
> dives opis natura suae, tu si modo recte
> dispensare velis ac non fugienda petendis
> immiscere.

> Say his Penis voiced his thoughts at such
> confusion: "I ask you! When I've reached my
> boiling point, do I ever ask for a vagina de-
> scended from dignified statesmen and dressed
> in a Lady's gown?" What would he answer?
> That she's a great sire's offspring? What a
> contrast and improvement is nature's own advice,
> full of resources; just steward them, and
> separate desirable practices from undesirable.

How wonderful that Villius (whoever he is) should be rebuked by his indignant member, much as Athens' Laws lecture Socrates in the *Crito* or Nature admonishes a fool in Lucretius' third book. The tone is exactly right, sound reinforces sense. A mock-heroic line illustrates the folly of snobbery in sexual matters and alliteration enhances the complaint. But here the fun stops. Horace retreats into School terminology, philosophical clichés. It is as though Sally Rand broke off in the middle of a striptease to lecture on "What Situation Ethics Can Mean to You."

Nor are humor and seriousness fully integrated in Satires I, 1. Horace seems uneasy, almost (in lines 23-27) apologetic about their relation. The true or "Socratic" seriocomic tone towards which he is drawn belongs to a conversational style more civilized and more personal than diatribe can provide.

A brief contrast will show his progress. In Satires I, 1, Horace depicted the folly of discontent and avarice (the latter rooted in the former) by conventional devices of diatribe, including anecdote, apostrophe, argument with a "straw man," and examples from the animal world. Consider the ant, says the speaker. She slaves all summer long, gathering grain, but in winter at least she profits from her toil: do you, from yours? The example is effective. Capitalists, not just sluggards, should "go to the ant." Then they might live more natural lives—a favorite moral of Hellenistic philosophy. Yet how much richer and more convincing is the mouse fable in Satires II, 6,[10] where the satirist no longer preaches to his congregation of fools from a superior position but laughs at folly as one who knows it personally: there but for good sense and a little luck go I!

Satires I, 2 and I, 1 have merit, or Horace would not have published them. Others are much better. Favorites, like I, 4, I, 6, and I, 9, have been analyzed well in recent years and praised for qualities developed in time and more impressive in Book 2: the cogent but informal presentation of an attitude or idea; the conversational tone, varied but harmonious; the appropriateness of diction, unobtrusiveness of transitions, use of guiding metaphors: in brief, their variety, unity, and control. Given these analyses, which will undoubtedly proliferate in the next decade, I wish to consider the Satires from another perspective, and show how closely Horace's reshaping of the genre is bound up with his personal growth, and especially with his regaining of a sense of rootedness in society.

II *Relocation in Society*

It is time we gave Maecenas proper credit for his contribution to Horace's growth as a writer and a man. The usual view is superficial. It goes like this. Maecenas, unlike Lord Chesterfield, came to the writer's aid when he was "struggling for life in the water" and liberated him, first with money, from the drudgery of the quaestor's clerkship, then, with the Sabine farm, from Rome itself. No strings were attached. If Horace, like Virgil, was pressured to write on Roman themes, he declined when he saw fit. Attendance at Maecenas' dinner parties was a more burdensome obligation. Horace gave Maecenas gratitude, companionship, and considerable moral support, and Maecenas is fortunate in being remembered as Horace's good patron, not the eccentric fool described by Seneca.[11]

This view gives Maecenas too much the advantage. He gets spiritual patronage for material, gold for brass. This is to overlook the pride and, more important, the understanding Horace gained from their association.

The pride is the more obvious. Horace valued solitude; he also enjoyed being designated a friend of Maecenas and "living with the great," as he called it later. He liked those dinner parties, less for the rich food than the company of men of affairs (not to mention other writers). For all his protestations to the contrary, he may have discussed political questions with Maecenas, as Swift did with Oxford and Bolingbroke on their brilliant Saturday afternoons. Sometimes, his satire seems clubbish, as when, in Satires I, 6, he pictures himself as belonging to a closed circle of reasonable men (lines 17-18):

> What should *we* then do, so far removed
> from the crowd?

or when, in Satires I, 9, he defines the standards of the group indirectly by satirizing an outsider, a tactless opportunist and bore, who prides himself on all the wrong literary and social qualities and imagines everyone else to be like himself. During the struggle (being aggressive, the man won't leave Horace alone, and being a bore, he is impervious to shafts of irony and only succumbs at the end to "divine intervention," a summons to court), Horace

praises the circle of Maecenas, mostly by indirection but once in a
dramatic explosion of indignation (lines 48-52):

> "We don't live there the way you think we
> do. No home's more true or sheltered from this
> dirt. It doesn't hurt me if Jones is richer than
> I or better educated: there's room for both."

The standards Horace upholds are thoroughly civilized, but there
is a touch of cruelty also.[12] The primitive community defines itself by expelling or killing a scapegoat. So, more subtly, do Shakespeare's Venetians, or their equivalents in present-day society.

More positively, however, Horace's relocation in society helped
him to personal fulfillment, a new acceptance of himself and others, and a corresponding redefinition of satiric purpose and style.
We forget how easily a sense of personal or social inadequacy may
cripple, though it intensifies, a poet's art and life. Sometimes
friendship and admiration do no good and he "expires," like
Swift, "a Driveller and a Show." Sometimes, however, they make
a difference. In the circle of Maecenas, Horace accepted his limitations and overcame them.

Comparison of Satires I, 6 with Epodes 4 shows a gain in perspective. Before, he raged at the opportunistic freedman. Now,
he rejects political ambition for himself, not without censuring
the mob that idiotically prefers ancestored dolts to intelligent and
honorable "Nobodies"; but he *also* ridicules the freedman's son
who rationalizes his unwarranted ambitions by pointing to the
man next down the line, the freedman Novius ("Newcomer").
This is precisely the delusion from which Horace has escaped,
thanks partly to Maecenas. He accepts disqualification from politics, praises his freedman father, and lyrically contrasts his quiet
everyday happiness with the burdensomeness and toil of a political
career. The symbolic radiance of leeks and peas, an oil flask and
saucer, anticipates imagery of happiness in the Odes. But Satires
I, 6 maintains what II, 6 lacks, a running satirical dichotomy between Horace and the fools, the sphere of sane thinking (here
identified with Maecenas' circle) and that of popular stupidity.
If the poet still protests a little too much about his freedom from
the "trap of sad ambition," any lingering dissatisfaction or feeling

of "sour grapes" will be exorcised—and rather more convincingly
—in Satires II, 6.

Maecenas' dinner parties did more than compensate for Horace's political ambitions. They made him feel no longer an aloof
spectator, but a responsible participant in society; they were a
"bridge to the world."[13] He puts down the preacher's mask, which
hardly suits a Roman dinner party; and while he remains a social
critic (for his claim, in Satires I, 4, that he writes just for self-improvement is evidently misleading), he now criticizes society from
within, as one who tolerates and supports his fellow men. As Sellar
has said, his enjoyment of social life helped provide "many materials of his art, and also the sanity of his genius, the moderation
and truth of his judgment, his immunity from the weaknesses and
extravagances of the literary temperament."[14]

His new position blends Socratic irony with Roman practicality.
For the Romans distrusted philosophical abstractions, just as they
took pride in their political superiority to the Greeks: a traditional, stable constitution beats all theoretical experiments (compare
Burke on the French Revolution). Just so, the horse sense that
Horace attributes to his father in Satires I, 4 makes the Schools
look rather silly (lines 115-120):

> "Professors will give you reasons for choosing
> x and avoiding y. It's enough for me to
> keep to the old ways and keep you safe, long
> as you need guarding, in life and reputation.
> Later, when time toughens your limbs and
> brain, you'll swim without the life-preserver."

The irony, the disrespect for professors, are of course Socratic as
well as Roman.

Horace never fully identified himself with the diatribe preacher. "Here endeth the lecture," he jokes at the conclusion of Satires
I, 1, and mocks the unwashed Stoic preacher whose beard urchins
love to tweak. And although Satires I, 3 has the diatribe form,
Horace denounces the Stoics in it for branding all men indiscriminately as sinners. Their paradox that "all sins are equal" is antisocial; if wisdom decrees intolerance, let us side (as Erasmus said
later) with Folly. Tolerance and forbearance are pillars of society.
Let us then be foolish in friendship, as lovers are blind, or par-

ents, to the faults of their loved ones; for those who most sharply scrutinize others' faults must expect the same hurtful treatment in return. The anecdote of the backbiter Maenius (lines 21-27) shows that satirists who live in glass houses should not throw stones. It also shows what, but for the grace of humor, Horace might have become.

His new awareness forces, not the end of diatribe, but its ironic containment. He appears now as the victim of preachers like Damasippus in Satires II, 3. Damasippus is an antique dealer who went bankrupt, contemplated suicide, was saved by a Stoic's reassurance that since everybody was mad, he need not feel ashamed of himself; so now he travels the lecture circuit with a convert's fanaticism. In bankrupt clichés, the proselytizer for Madmen Anonymous bends Horace's ear on the subject "all fools are mad," including (a) misers, (b) spendthrifts, (c) politicians, (d) lovers, (e) superstitious people, and especially (f) Horace, who is extravagant, ill-tempered, and lustful! The diatribe, though smelling of the manual, is lively and amusing; but the greatest joke is of course on (g) the Mad Satirist himself. And there, but for his understanding, goes Horace.

Again, in Satires II, 7, Horace has his diatribe and ridicules it too. Here the slave Davus lectures on the paradox that "all fools are slaves." While many of his shots go ludicrously wild (Horace is *not* a consummate glutton and lecher), others approach the mark, and we are to laugh at Horace's annoyance when he is attacked as inconsistent (lines 28-30):

> In Rome you want the country, there you
> praise Rome to the skies. When you're
> invited nowhere to dinner, you praise
> Carefree Vegetables.

The compliment to Maecenas is genuine, but so is the self-criticism. Vegetables are not as romantic as Satires II, 6 makes them appear, nor are discontent and inconsistency easily mastered. For all that, Davus remains the slave, not Horace; not only by fortune, but because his mentality is hidebound and slavish in its dogmatism. Only the humorous self-awareness that Stoics so seldom manifest gives the inner freedom, from vain imaginings, that Stoics so much discuss.

If the later satires ring with a free man's laughter, Horace's re-conciliation with society helped create this freedom. He repaid society and his patron by writing socially accountable satire. By so doing, he surrendered the prophetic stance of the satirist who judges society from without, denouncing it as corrupt and sinful. He would not be a Juvenal or Swift. What he gained by includ-ing himself, as he had been and was, in the ship of fools, was a com-ic perspective that helped him become what he wanted to be: a genuine "freedman" like his father.

III   Redefinition of Satire

The circle of Maecenas partially coincides with the circle of Vir-gil, as we might call that group of poets and critics who shaped Augustan standards of craftsmanship after Philippi. What en-couragement they gave one another, we can only guess, but Horace himself pays tribute to the severity of their mutual criticism:

> "Change this, and this," Quintilius used to
> say when you recited. You couldn't do better?
> You'd tried it many times? "Destroy it then.
> Your lathe's no good, start over with your
> hammer." If you chose to defend your crime,
> not change it, not a word more, he'd not waste
> effort. You could admire yourself in splendid
> isolation.[15]

The standards were high. Messalla and Pollio demanded purest "Latinity." Virgil revised ceaselessly; on his deathbed he ordered the Aeneid burned rather than published in what he considered its imperfect state; but Augustus, fortunately, countermanded the order, and Virgil's executors, Varius Rufus and Plotius Tucca, edited and published the Aeneid with minor changes. *Tantae molis erat*—"such labor it took."

This group, we notice first, maintained independence of ex-pression and judgment through the civil wars. Horace's list in Satires I, 10 of men for whom he writes embraces both camps, Oc-tavian's and Antony's. Second, there is no quarrel between Augus-tans and Neoterics: the standards of the Thirties continue those of the Fifties, Horace's insistence on brevity and polish is thoroughly Catullan, and the poetasters he satirizes correspond to the "toilet-paper writers" lampooned by Catullus. Even Virgil, at whose epic ambitions the Neoterics would have shuddered, began in a minor, "subtle" genre, like a would-be architect apprenticed to an engraver or watchmaker. Third, for the Augustans, as for Catullus and his coterie, literary and social standards coincided. To Catullus, stealing napkins and writing bad verse are equally criminal forms of behavior; so, to Horace, are overwriting and social climbing. To both, your "severest critic" was indeed your "best friend," for he cured your weaknesses by exposing them; whereas the flatterer confirms you in faults and makes you a laughingstock. As Catullus calls his friends *faceti* and *urbani,* implying the traits of wit and sophistication that drew them together, Horace calls Virgil and Varius *candidi*: honest men and good. It was they, significantly, who introduced him to *"candide Maecenas."*

A brake on harshness was the Epicurean training that Virgil, Varius, Plotius, and Quintilius received in the Forties, when they fled to the "safe harbor" of Siro in Naples. Virgil broke later with Epicureanism; so, perhaps, did the others; but like ex-seminarians they must have retained many marks of their training. Mutual correction, gentle but firm, was a chief Epicurean principle.[16] Philodemus, the Epicurean philosopher who lived at Herculaneum, wrote a treatise on free speech; his admonitions essentially resemble St. Paul's. The Roman students, to whom Philodemus dedicated other treatises, as yet unrecovered, on flattery and on frankness, learned to be honest without being tactless or unkind.

Horace himself never studied with Siro, but the Epicurean tone rubbed off on him. Thus Satires I, 6, to Maecenas, joins frankness with respect, and gratitude with honest pride: a fine and lasting combination. At the same time, formation of right tone bears directly on satire. Lucilius, whom Horace followed, saw himself as an arbiter of good taste, of a style of life based on moral and philosophical conceptions and variously expressed in conversation and dress, poetry, politics, and dinner parties. He defended that style through the positive example of his life and writings, and he attacked those who deviated from it in whatever area.

If the differences between Lucilius and Horace have obscured more important similarities, that is Horace's fault. He had to solve a two-sided problem. Since Roman "satire" traditionally meant a literary medley or potpourri (the name being derived from "stuffing" or a raisin pudding), he had to give shape to an essentially formless genre—the only one, said Quintilian, that was wholly Roman; but also, while adopting Lucilian verse satire (as against the "Menippean" mixture of verse and prose written by Ennius and Varro), he had to escape the *character Lucilianus,* the stamp of aggressiveness and invective by which Lucilian satire was marked in the popular mind. In that struggle, Horace did injustice to Lucilius, whose satire was a brilliant and original creation. If Puelma Piwonka is right, Lucilius succeeded in subordinating the techniques of Greek popular philosophy, as seen in the diatribe of Bion of Borysthenes, to a personal and ironic conversational form, susceptible of great variety and freshness (as the diatribe is not); but at the same time, though influenced by Callimachus, he did not aim like the Hellenistic poets at art for art's sake, but at social and moral—that is, Roman—effectiveness.[17] His satire is then, like Plautine comedy (which Horace never appreciated), a fine bastard form, combining Greek conceptions and Roman practicality, individual self-fulfillment and political devotion: in short, a Hellenistic and a classical ideal.

Ironically, Horace's criticisms of Lucilius are descended from Lucilius' criticisms of second-century epic and tragic poets, his standards are fundamentally the same, and his title, *sermones* ("conversations"), comes from Lucilius. Ironically, too, the further he defines his individual style and purpose, the more he appreciates Lucilius and places his own writing in the "satiric" tradition[18]—much as a son best acknowledges his parents after they have ceased to dominate his personality.

The change is clear, as Fraenkel has shown. In Satires I, 4, Lucilius is portrayed as a Roman Primitive, undiscriminating in diction and meter, ignorant of true *libertas,* or free satiric speech. The satirist, says Horace, should not harass evildoers without provocation like a censor or informer. While Lucilius contrasted his role of *censor morum* with the irresponsible backbiting of the *dicax,* or "wit," Horace goes further. Not only is he an honest friend, as Lucilius professed himself: he rejects the intention of giving pain, which assists neither self-reformation nor the improvement of society. Posterity will not then confuse him with the Mad Satirist, as it did Lucilius.

After writing Satires I, 4, Horace was attacked by self-constituted champions of Lucilius—ironically, the kind of philological Establishment that Terence and Lucilius resisted in the Scipionic period. In Satires I, 10, he redefines his satiric mode, still contrasting it to that of Lucilius (lines 9-15):

> Be brief, so your thought may run, not hamper
> itself with words overpowering tired ears;
> be solemn sometimes, oftentimes amusing; stand
> duty, now for the orator and poet, now for the
> wit who spares his energy and sharpens it to
> a point. Humor can cut through great affairs
> keener than sarcasm.

Flexibility, not vehemence, holds the reader's attention. Horace can change roles. Witness Satires II, 3 and II, 7, where, as we saw, the Mad Satirist is controlled dramatically; indeed, the over-all variety of Book II is due mainly to the role-shifting power of the satirist and the plasticity of hexameter verse that ranges from mock-heroic solemnity to a simulation of everyday low conversation. Yet, Horace concedes, Lucilius was not only the Firstcomer (*inventor*) to this satiric form; he adhered in principle to the same ironic, Socratic style, only his practice fell short (lines 64-71):

> Lucilius, I grant you, had an agreeable wit and
> somewhat more polish than most creators of an
> untried poetic form, untouched by the Greeks;[19] more
> too than your older crowd of poets; still, say fate
> had carried him down to our time, he'd exercise his
> file, and prune what trailed excessively; writing
> verses, he'd often scratch his head and bite his
> nails to the quick.

Literary standards are relative. Lucilius was witty—for his time. In Horace's he would have written less casually, would have built on Neoteric example and on Cicero's refinement of the plain-style theory in rhetoric.

The hint that Horace is Lucilius reborn (he would say, *repraesentatus*)[20] is carried further in Satires II, 1. Here Trebatius, a worried lawyer-friend, advises him not to write satire. Why not praise Octavian's virtue and might, as Lucilius praised Scipio's?

Horace declines, but later admits to "following" Lucilius in confiding personal experience to satire (lines 30-34):

> He trusted private thoughts to his writings, as
> to intimate friends, went running nowhere else
> if something came off badly or turned out well:
> that's why the old man's life is revealed as plain
> as the scene on a votive tablet. I'm for his
> footsteps.

Most votive tablets are, as Anderson remarks, quite coarse.[21] Horace kept no rough diary, wrote no Romantic confessions. He does, however, acknowledge Lucilius' precedence here in more than form. Satire represents a way of life.

Recapitulation of this theme is forestalled by an ironic defense of satire. Horace writes by instinct, as others drink, dance, box, or ride. It helps him sleep. Furthermore, his satire is a defensive weapon only. His admission (for the first time) that he has, and can exert, the power of wolf or bull, is modified by what preceded; for in full perspective, satire writing is just another foible or sport, a way of filling time, Dr. Johnson would say, as pardonable as card playing.

Then Trebatius' last warning, that writing satire may still get Horace in trouble, leads to a recapitulation of both themes, play-quarrel and Horace's relation to Lucilius (lines 62-78):

> Now, when Lucilius first dared put together
> poems in this fashion, stripping the hide from
> men who then paraded sleek and shining, but
> filthy underneath, did Laelius or the man who
> got his name from Carthage's destruction take
> offense when that proud intellect wounded
> Metellus and buried Lupus under a mighty pile
> of scurrilous verses? No: he rushed the
> people, chief by chief and tribe by tribe,
> before the judgment seat of Laughter, fair to
> virtue alone and virtue's friends. And yet,
> when Scipio, that parfit knyght, and Laelius,
> that font of wisdom, drew apart to privacy,
> they'd loose their belts and sport with him
> until the greens were cooked.

> Now take myself—in brain and place way
> underneath the great Lucilius: still, envy
> must admit I too have lived with the great,
> and bite, surprised, upon that solid truth.

The differences stand out. They were meant to. As a knight and Scipio's friend, Lucilius flayed "Wolf" and other enemies with impunity. Horace lacks that aristocratic certainty, that Old Roman zest for picking quarrels. He possesses, however, Lucilius' equally great power of relaxation, of playing and conversing with Rome's leaders under the rules of leisure. It is an enviable position.

His new social confidence, and the unity of idea and feeling underlying his renovation of Lucilian satire, are summarized in a splendid pun. Trebatius is still worried. As a lawyer, he represents society's claims on the individual. But Horace reassures him (lines 78-84):

> Unless, my learned friend Trebatius, you
> disagree? "No, I don't see a loophole; still
> be advised: take care; lack of acquaintance
> with our time-honored laws may cause you
> trouble: 'IF ONE CREATE BAD CHARMS AGAINST
> ANOTHER, BE HE BOUND UNTO COURT.'" So be it.
> But, what if one create some *charming poems
> bound* to be praised at *court*?[22]

It is a nice quibble. The implications are clear: "good poetry" is its own best defense; and anyway, under Octavian's protection, Horace could write, if he chose, with Lucilian impunity. But more: the "laws" of the genre reflect, in the good taste they require, those of society, and have developed along with them.

Originally, the law against *mala carmina* concerned witchcraft, not libel. It reflected the view of the satirist held by primitive peoples, which Robert Elliott has described.[23] The archetypal satirist is a magician, an enemy of the people. He may sometimes be socially useful, even lead armies into battle; but his power to wound and blight with words makes him uncontrollable, a latent menace at best, and at worst an open blackmailer and terrorist like Aithirne the Importunate. As Elliott says, psychological explanations of the satirist's power make little difference. He had it: raised welts of shame, drove proud men to suicide (compare the story of Archilochus and Lycambes). Less primitive ages, we might add, are not always consistently rational in such matters. Charles Williams cites the attempts of ninth-century French bishops to discourage both sorcery and belief in sorcery.[24] Would any satirist worth his salt admit that witch-hunting has disappeared in modern times? When Horace wrote, in an age which by his own evidence was fairly superstitious, the imprecise libel law was not only derived from the ancient law against witchcraft: to an extent, it still *was* the old law, still expressed the popular conviction that the satirist wields a demonic antisocial power. In asserting, therefore, that he writes *bona carmina*, Horace means more than that they are well-written and nonlibelous. They are white magic, power exerted for good. Later, in Epistles I, 1, he will advertise the Socratic "incantations" (the metaphor is Plato's) by which mental ills are healed.

One way civilization defines itself is by revisiting the primitive. Ever since Odysseus entered Polyphemus' cave, poets, historians, and novelists have been showing how recent and how thin the veil of civilization is. In a like manner literature may become conscious of its own development. In Satires I, 5, among other comic incidents of his Trip to Brundisium, Horace describes the entertainment furnished by a brace of clowns (lines 56-64; I am paraphrasing):

> Sarmentus: "I say you're like a wild horse."
> Messius Cicirrus: "Okay, then!" (threatening
>   motion with his head.)
> Sarm: "Lucky they cut your horn out. You're
>   still a monstrous, mutilated menace."
> (Messius Cicirrus had an ugly scar on the left
> side of his shaggy face, so the jokes came
> fast and thick. What a mug! Did he have the
> Campanian pox? Why didn't he do the Cyclops'
> Dance—after all, he wouldn't need a
> mask! . . .)

From such improvised contests art is born. Indeed, Johan Huizinga has shown that many of our social, juridical, and philosophical institutions evolved from play forms akin to the Eskimo "drumming matches" and the contests of the Plains Indians in hooting and jeering.[25] Primitive humor is gross. It plays on animal comparisons, physical challenge, and sexual insult, and it is still very funny if we can forget our inhibitions momentarily. But the gulf between Sarmentus and Horace shows how far satire had developed by then (for the laughter of Maecenas' company is largely based on their own rather cruel sense of superiority to the clowns). It also shows the continuity of the impulse by which satire was first produced.

Today we can relate the development of satire to that of comedy with more perspective than Horace had. Imagine a first stage in which the satirist, wild, dangerous, and somewhat mad, lampoons an individual who is (to pursue one example) stingy. Since stinginess is a blighting force in the community, the satirist symbolically kills the man or expels him from society to preserve the fertility of women and crops. The victim may in fact run away or commit suicide. In our hypothetical second stage, invective becomes art. When Aristophanes composes majestic imprecations against a producer who dined his chorus meagerly, he is not employing black magic or excommunicating the offender in any real sense. His exaggeration gives emotional relief but aims chiefly at its own artistic perfection. If producers give better dinners henceforth, that is all to the good. In the third stage, a stingy individual is no longer singled out for caricature. Instead, the vice of avarice is typified in the stock miser, whose obsession makes him a ridiculous, mechanical, perhaps pathetic figure (see Bergson's fine analysis of this type of humor, which Horace often employs). But notice that, along with the Miser, the "New Comedy" or "Comedy of Manners" also casts out—or better, invites *into* society—the misanthrope or "ill-tempered man" who has rejected society because of its vices. We observed earlier what importance this addition had to Horace's satire. He is, like Lucilius, a product of all three stages; but more decisively than Lucilius, he rejects the first stage and tempers the second with the third, combining "Eupolis and Archilochus, Plato and Menander" (as he describes his bookshelf).[26] The blend proved excellent. Others were to follow, responding to time and temperament, reacting against the classical and seeking it again. Persius and Juvenal, Dryden and Pope.

Horace may never have appreciated Lucilius adequately. One reason was the pain that sloppy hexameters and muddled diction gave him. Another was the resentment he felt all his life against the entrenched philologians who, from envy, he thought, of their contemporaries, magnified the importance of the Ancients they explicated out of all proportion. Yet he became gradually aware that he owed more than a formal debt to the satiric tradition established by Lucilius. The more surely he defined his personal goals, the more he felt at home in that tradition. We are faced here with the classical paradox of continuity through transformation. Every forward thrust in art and thought means the death of what went before. Sons and students rebel; they must, in order to grow; and sometimes, they are disinherited; yet their rebellion only continues the creative work, which was itself rebellion, of their fathers and teachers before them. That is why Lucilius' editors showed themselves fools when they attacked Horace, for they were attacking the master's flesh and blood and defending a lifeless shadow.

IV *Renewal of Spirit*

There is another, less tangible side of Horace's transformation of satire. This is Virgil's spiritual guidance, the action of a visionary and dreamer on a practical man.

In Satires I, 10, Horace sets satire alongside pastoral. Both are contrasted with the "high" genres, epic and tragedy. Virgil's form is characterized as *molle atque facetum*, "sensitive and sophisticated"; the latter applies to satire as well. Satires I, 10 closes a book arranged like the Eclogues: poems 4-6 as central, flanked by 1-3 and 7-9; 10 as epilogue. But Virgil's influence can be seen in less outward ways: in the pastoral terms in which Horace describes his leisurely existence in Satires I, 6 (*pererro, vagor*: he "wanders, browsing" like a goat), and in the prayer to Mercury in Satires II, 6, 14-15,

> pingue pecus domino facias et cetera praeter
> ingenium.
>
> (Fatten my flock and livelihood, but keep
> my spirit thin.)

which recalls Virgil's *recusatio* or "refusal" in Eclogue 6, 3-8:

> cum canerem reges et proelia, Cynthius aurem
> vellit et admonuit: "pastorem, Tityre, pinguis
> pascere oportet ovis, deductum dicere carmen."
> nunc ego (namque super tibi erunt qui dicere laudes,
> Vare, tuas cupiant et tristia condere bella)
> agrestem tenui meditabor harundine Musam.

> (When I was chanting kings and battle scenes,
> Cynthius plucked my ear and said, "Shepherds
> should fatten sheep at pasture, Tityrus,
> but sing a slender song."
> Others will praise you, Varus, and your warfare
> set down bravely in measure: I will practice
> a woodland music with my slender pipe.)

As Virgil adhered to the "slender" or "subtle" style of poetry and life (Greek *leptos*, Latin *tenuis*), Horace too chose "plain living and high thinking"—tested, to be sure, by the City Mouse, and at length reaffirmed: *tenui solabitur ervo.* Humorously, self-consciously, with a certain intentional coarseness, he appropriated Virgil's pastoral vision for himself.

To go back a decade, to the beginning of their lifelong dialogue: there are allusions in Epode 16 to Eclogue 4—or is it the other way around? The famous "priority question" will never be solved to everyone's satisfaction. In fact, it is unimportant. What matters is a disagreement of outlook. Even if Eclogue 4 is, as some have argued and I believe, an optimistic response to Epode 16, Horace may still have taken issue with other eclogues, from which Virgil's grand prophecy of the world's renewal differs less in spirit than is generally imagined.

Basically, the disagreement is about the meaning of escape. Horace's epode ends with a wish-fulfillment daydream that expresses his disillusionment with Roman history. It begins despairingly, with a recollection of Hesiod's myth, the Decline of the Ages:

> altera iam teritur bellis civilibus aetas,

> (Another age in civil war is now worn down,)

Gold tarnishes, men die. The Iron Age is upon us. So Horace calls an assembly and summons an honorable, courageous remnant to flee with him (the last word is *fuga*, "flight") to the Rich Islands where the Golden Age is miraculously preserved.

Horace utterly despairs of Rome. Hence the unrealistic proposal, the contrast between the blessed islands and Roman reality. Some fifteen years earlier, Catullus, disillusioned by Lesbia's treachery and the general corruption of the time, drew a similar contrast (in poem 64) between an idealized heroic past and a decadent, godless present. Horace is nostalgic like Catullus; he longs for a happier time, now lost, for Rome and himself (it was a year since Philippi, and new wars were beginning); so he takes on the prophet's role and summons men—to retreat into an inner world of the imagination. Only there is happiness possible. A variation of the same attitude appears in the earliest satires, whose detached cynicism is idealism reversed.

Virgil's call to escape is different.[27] He never wilfully cuts himself off from reality. For him, as for Theocritus before him, the masque of the singing shepherds is rather a metaphor of return, from the superficiality of ordinary life, especially as lived in the metropolis, to deeper realities of human and natural existence. His descriptions of a countryside half in Italy, half in fairyland, convey a joy of spirit that transcends possessions, places, even security: for if Virgil in Eclogue I is Tityrus, the shepherd who retains his creative leisure as by a divine gift, he is also Meliboeus, the shepherd uprooted from his lands and driven into exile, who can nonetheless be touched, if only a little, by the sympathetic, healing power of nature and of natural feeling. Yet in a mysterious way Virgil's inwardness of joy implies an outward movement, a sympathetic feeling of relatedness to the whole of reality. The ordinary historical facts—Octavian's patronage, confiscation of property, murderous veterans—are drawn into and harmonized within the idealizing world of the imagination. This is no escapist daydream. It is an irradiation of life by the spirit, implied in Eclogue 1, and come to fullest flower in the grand prophecy of Eclogue 4, in which the Georgics and Aeneid are anticipated.

Horace was touched, though never fully convinced by the pastoral vision. He translated the two sides of Virgilian *otium*, interior joy and relatedness to the whole of life, into terms appropriate to his own temperament and literary forms. We saw in Satires II, 6 how happiness lay in a mental state of acceptance.[28] Similarly, in Epode 2, any false note of escapism in the praise of country happiness is undercut, both by a slight but sure exaggeration of rural joys throughout the poem, and by the surprise ending in which Alfius, the moneylender (for that is who has been singing the countryside's praises), finishes—by running back to Wall Street. The poem is "sensitive and sophisticated." Horace loves the Sabine farm, but not, he knows, with Virgil's purity of motivation: that is why he must exorcize with ironic humor whatever in himself resembles Alfius or the City Mouse.

In his beloved Sabine retreat he also relates himself, like Virgil, to the whole of life, turning his back on that earlier self that escaped, or wished to escape, into uncaring isolation: that is, into unreality. As Satires II, 1 shows him rooted once more in a Roman tradition and Roman surroundings, Epode 1, to Maecenas, shows him concerned again with Roman history. Concerned, not necessarily happy. Although he takes a *sacramentum* or oath of allegiance to Maecenas[29] and follows him to Actium, as Maecenas followed Octavian, he proves more diffident than exultant as the battle leans to victory.[30] Epode 9 expresses "nausea," disgust with the war, not just anxiety about its outcome. Yet Horace's presence at Actium showed more than personal loyalty to Maecenas. As he says of the Ship of State in an allegorical ode, I, 14, written soon after Actium, it was

> nuper sollicitum quae mihi taedium,
> nunc desiderium curaque non levis:
>
> (Before, I felt harassment and disgust;
> now, a lover's desire, no light concern.)

Epodes 2 and 1, like Satires II, 6, complete one stage of Horace's work. Neither form was exhausted, as the variety of the Epodes and Satires II attests. In the Epistles, Horace would revive the *sermo* form. But the Satires and Epodes were more than literary accomplishments, recreating a Greek and a Latin genre: they also were expressions of a personality that outgrew forms even as it renewed them. As Eliot wrote about Joyce,

[*43*]

One of the greatest capabilities of genius is the power of development. The value of a man's work should correspond to this capacity in him: what he leaves behind should be no more and no less than what is needed to realize each definite stage of his development.[31]

Though more a reflection on his own work than universally applicable, Eliot's statement is appropriate to Virgil and Horace. Neither "pastured his goats" too long, both knew that "too much shade harms the fruits." An inner need drove Horace to lyric as it drove Virgil to epic. There is, significantly, no overlapping of Satires and Odes. The one book was completed and published. The other was begun.

CHAPTER 3

The Alcaean Lyre[1]

I A Double Perspective

TO imitate Alcaeus' lyrics without loss of originality was a new and complex task. Horace had not only to domesticate Aeolic and other meters; he had once more to revive the classical spirit within a predominantly Hellenistic culture. His chief model, Alcaeus, had been actively engaged in the politics of the late seventh and early sixth centuries; his very drinking songs embody aristocratic party feeling. Hellenistic poets, on the other hand, like Theocritus and Callimachus, were uprooted from their natural soil of political life under the dynasts who succeeded Alexander the Great. They were thrown back on literary companionship and private resources of the spirit. Ordinary men could cling to the mystery religions for comfort in a rapidly expanding, cosmopolitan civilization, or learn from the new Stoic and Epicurean schools of philosophy how to become independent and self-sufficient. Roman tradition, it is true, stressed different values: self-abnegation, loyalty to the state. But Rome was caught up in the dynastic struggles of the late third and early second centuries; and although the Middle Stoa accommodated its principles to Roman practice and, emphasizing the ethics of duty and propriety, became almost an established philosophy under the younger Scipio, individualism proved (as Cato had warned) to be a highly contagious disease. In the politics of Pompey and Caesar, the poetry of Catullus, and the Epicurean philosophy of Lucretius and many others, it dominated the late Republic in the Sixties, Fifties, and Forties. Cicero fought on all fronts for Roman tradition and died, with the Republic, in 43 B.C. How, then, after Actium (for Antony's death in 31 B.C. ends the Hellenistic Age, as Alexander's in 323 B.C. began it), could "sensitive and sophisticated" Roman poets regain the older sense of community? How restore meaning to the old lesson, still instinctive in many Romans, that the state came first?

Horace probably saw the two problems, technical and spiritual, as being somehow connected. His regularization, for example, of caesura and quantity (the long fourth syllable) in the Sapphic meter,[2]

Persicos odi, puer, apparatus,

consorts well with the surprising moral seriousness of Odes I, 38. The poem may be classified formally as a variant on the species known as invitation poem.[3] These were common in Hellenistic epigram, and generally lightweight. Philodemus writes such an epigram to amuse his patron, Piso—and requests some extra cash; Catullus, with finer irony and in a lyrical meter, conveys his deep personal affection for a friend. But Horace's ode, though slight in form and subject matter, is what the others are not: a classical *paideia* in miniature.

Again, Horace's metrical innovations give his Alcaic stanza the dramatic movement and responsion that Gilbert Murray described. "The last verse," he said, "is extraordinarily delightful in rhythm, but it would be nothing in particular if it were not reached by a struggle—and just the right kind of a struggle."[4] Examples will be given later. But Murray's statement holds true, precisely, for Horace's moral wisdom.

Alcaic, Sapphic, and Asclepiadic meters: Horace shaped them all to his purposes; and in Frost's words, "the possibilities of tune from the dramatic tones of meaning strung across the rigidity of a limited meter are endless."[5] Our main concern, however, is with Horace's spiritual relation to Alcaeus. Classicists have learned, especially from that great and humane scholar, Georgio Pasquali, with what freedom Horace adapted Alcaeus: how he mixes classical motifs with Hellenistic, or begins with a borrowed phrase like *nunc est bibendum* ("Now we must drink!" in the Cleopatra ode, I, 37) and continues where he pleases. But Pasquali, like many scholars, saw no possibility of reconciliation between "the artist who dispassionately contemplates beauty and the Roman citizen who holds to the ancient ideals, revived now by the Emperor's will." The single ode, he felt, had artistic unity; an intentional disharmony ruled the collection.[6] Was Pasquali right? Or may we say, with Klingner, that in returning to classical models Horace found a means of overcoming the Hellenistic split between the private and public worlds?[7] The question is crucial to our understanding of Horace's poetry, especially his political odes; for not only his art but the integrity of his imagination is at stake.

An early ode, I, 26, weds Alcaic measures to the native rhythm of the Latin language with almost complete success. It also dramatizes a tentative outward movement of the poet from a secure, private world, set apart by symbolic boundaries from foreign concerns, to friendship and the giving of a present.

> Musis amicus tristitiam et metus
> tradam protervis in mare Creticum
>   portare ventis, quis sub Arcto
>   rex gelidae metuatur orae,
>
> quid Tiridaten terreat, unice
> securus. o quae fontibus integris
>   gaudes, apricos necte flores,
>   necte meo Lamiae coronam,
>
> Piplei dulcis! nil sine te mei
> prosunt honores: hunc fidibus novis,
>   hunc Lesbio sacrare plectro
>   teque tuasque decet sorores.
>
> (Muses befriend me. Sadness and fear I'll
> order the playful winds to blow into the
> Cretan sea. Whose scepter is feared in the
> icy North, what Tiridates dreads, is not my
> concern. Dear Muse, who rejoice in untouched
> springs, interweave your sunlit flowers for
> Lamia. Alone, I cannot consecrate him on the
> Lesbian lyre and new quill: that is your and
> your sisters' right.)

The metaphor of the untouched springs recalls Callimachus' stylistic program, his refusal to treat common themes in the ordinary way. Long before Callimachus, however, Hesiod had been consecrated by the Muses, and Pindar had used honey, water, and wine as symbols of the creativity a poet enjoys and the power of refreshment he communicates. Not only do Horace and Virgil fulfill Hellenistic standards of originality by transcending Hellenistic limitations of form and returning to Homer and the older lyric poets: they also experience in their lives a kind of rhythm by which withdrawal into poetic isolation implies a corresponding movement outwards, towards public sharing and public effectiveness. The weaving of the garland, always an Horatian signature, is also a classical metaphor. Here it illustrates, not only the marriage of Alcaic form and Latin rhythm, but also an intuition of the possibility of spiritual return, from withdrawal to participation.

But if Horace tentatively reaches toward classicism in Odes I, 26, he rears away from it in I, 6, to Agrippa. Varius, he says, will celebrate your victory in Homeric song; I myself am simply not up to such great subjects, to epic or tragedy. "Modesty and my peaceful lyric Muse" warn me not to spoil everything. No: rather than sing of wars,

> nos convivia, nos proelia virginum
> sectis in iuvenes unguibus acrium
> cantamus vacui, sive quid urimur
>   non praeter solitum leves.

> (*I* sing of feasts, fierce maidens fighting with
> fingernails against their lovers—but uninvolved;
> even aflame, my heart is easy and peaceful.)

The poem is a *recusatio*, one of many "refusals" by Virgil, Horace, and the elegists to write historical or panegyrical epics, especially on Actium. In metaphors that quickly became trite—the untouched spring, the untrodden path, the prohibition by Apollo or some other literary-minded divinity—Callimachus had rejected such epics because their form was unwieldy and their subject matter trite. They were anachronistic, he felt; they defied originality of treatment; they competed with Homer; they mixed history with mythology, to the advantage of neither. Yet epic was not unthinkable in terms of Augustan craftsmanship.[8] When Horace wrote, Varius had completed one epic and Virgil, after smuggling history into pastoral and didactic poetry, was beginning another—

on Aeneas, to be sure, not Actium. When Horace, therefore, like Propertius after him, refuses to celebrate Octavian's deeds, his reasons are personal. He is unable, or unwilling, to sustain the burden of a proper epic poem. He may also be hinting that the subject matter disagrees with him. Octavian and Agrippa recently showed themselves as "stubborn," "treacherous," and "ferocious" as the Greek heroes to whom (in the epic manner!) they are here compared. Horace's imagination therefore recoils, as it did in Epode 16, from the brutality and evil of civil war into a sphere of freedom from emotional involvement; for the world of drinking and lovemaking is happily free from commitment once it is controlled by the ironic attitude suggested in *tenues* and *leves*. Odes I, 6 ends precisely where I, 26 began, in a sheltered world.

A comparable flight can be seen in Odes II, 1, where anticipation of Pollio's history sharpens Horace's memories of civil war. He still hears the trumpets, sees the great generals falling in the dust. The world runs blood; so (lines 37-40):

> sed ne relictis, Musa procax, iocis
> Ceae retractes munera neniae,
>   mecum Dionaeo sub antro
>   quaere modos leviore plectro.

> (Leave not fooling, my forward Muse;
> Cean dirges are not your style;
>   striking more softly, move into
>   Venus' cave.)

By thus recalling his Muse to her rightful province of erotic, playful poetry (hence the double entendres), Horace is not just reminding himself, or us, that the tragic-historic vision must be qualified by other views of life. His wilful discontinuity of thought suggests an emotional reaction. War is horrible: better escape into a gentler world. Of course, the reaction is itself a tribute to Pollio, for the business of the great historian is not merely to explain the past, but to make us feel it. Still, the "lightness" of lyric poetry in the hierarchical scale of genres serves here, as in I, 6, to justify the very split in poetic consciousness that, according to Klingner, Horace's choice of Alcaeus as model and guide helped him to overcome.

This is not to revive the "two Horaces" nonsense. No poet suffered less from schizophrenia. The Alcaean lyre, however, which in its master's hands knew no distinction between private and public song, seems to have suggested two possibilities to Horace. He could take a borderline position, as in Odes I, 6, flirting with political themes but withdrawing at will into an apolitical world; or he could achieve what Odes I, 26 seems to intimate, a reunification of the two worlds that would do injustice to neither. Perhaps the real point of the *recusatio* lies, as Wimmel has suggested, in its power to gain time for the creative poet.[9] His increasing maturity in turn influences his conception of how he is related to his literary models. We saw in the previous chapter how the independence Horace achieved in satire brought him closer in spirit to Lucilius. Similarly, his decision to follow Alcaeus, his early intuition of the unifying power of classical lyric poetry over Hellenistic and Roman experience, gains new meaning from a few years of poetic experimentation and thought. What Horace made of the Alcaean lyre corresponds very closely to what, in those same years, he made of himself.

II *Boundaries of Conduct*

The notion of limit runs through Horace's poetry like a red thread. Meaning lies in measure: in *modus*, which refers, often simultaneously, to the means of achieving a goal, the rhythm and harmony found in music, and the right limit of human conduct; in *finis*, the "boundary" or goal of choice (Cicero called his treatise on ethics *De Finibus*); and in *mediocritas*, the Aristotelian mean between vicious extremes in behavior. Our instinctive resistance today to the idea of the "Golden Mean" (*aurea mediocritas*) owes its strength to Romanticism, to a linguistic debasement of the words "mean" and "mediocre," and to the separation of Horace's moral generalizations from the poetry in which they are rooted. All this has ruined Horace for many readers.

We must not ignore Horace's search for right *meaning* in life, which accompanies his effort to achieve right *measure* in poetry. His wisdom ripened through experience, like his poetry. To have been born mature would have been most improper, and Horace disliked impropriety. The classical wisdom, therefore, that he inherits and reshapes is given final meaning and universality by qualities only acquired in time: responsiveness to the concrete situation, as it constantly changes with every person and moment; and a sympathetic and penetrating grasp of the workings of human emotion.

Compare an early satire to an early ode, and the difference will be plain. In Satires I, 1, the satirist dictated a practical limit to moneymaking that would equally be removed from the other extreme of squandering wealth (lines 92-94, 106-107):

> denique sit finis quaerendi, cumque habeas plus
> pauperiem metuas minus, et finire laborem
> incipias, . . .

> Est modus in rebus, sunt certi denique fines,
> quos ultra citraque nequit consistere rectum.

> (Limit your love of acquisition. When you get
> more, fear poverty less, and begin to set bounds
> to your labor. . . .

> Limit exists in things, and certain bounds
> outside of which right conduct cannot stand.)

In Odes I, 7, Horace makes a similar recommendation but in less abstract and scholastic language. He is addressing a real person, his friend Munatius Plancus, who was apparently depressed by a prolonged absence from home (lines 15-19):

> albus ut obscuro deterget nubila caelo
>   saepe Notus neque parturit imbris
> perpetuo, sic tu sapiens finire memento
>   tristitiam vitaeque labores
> molli, Plance, mero. . . .

> (As the South Wind oft sweeps the clouds
> away from a dark sky, and showers descend
> not everlastingly, be wise, and limit
> labor and lamentation, Plancus, with
> mellow draughts of wine. . . .)

The act of drinking here exemplifies a sensible attitude toward life. Plancus should make the best of things, live independently of place and fortune, and face the future as unworried as was the

/0//62

hero, Teucer, before he sailed for a new Salamis. At the same time, the raising of the wine cup is an irrational gesture, an acceptance of fate—or a way of keeping it at bay. "Drive out cares with wine!" cries Teucer; "Tomorrow we sail again on the great sea" (lines 31-32):

> nunc vino pellite curas;
> cras ingens iterabimus aequor.

Sense and emotion are perilously balanced here. The "solution" to Plancus' troubles is not very philosophical or sure, but it is the best Horace has to offer.

Although, from one striking phrase, Horace is remembered as poet of the "Golden Mean," good sense never in itself produces good poetry, and some early odes in praise of moderation are relatively uninteresting. Thus, in Odes II, 18, Horace stands apart, a detached spectator of what his inverse counterpart, the faceless *tu*, does or suffers (lines 17-22):

> tu secanda marmora
> locas sub ipsum funus et sepulcri
>   immemor struis domos
> marisque Bais obstrepentis urges
>   summovere litora,
> parum locuples continente ripa.

> (At death's own door you take contractors'
> estimates for cutting marble; unmindful of
> the tomb, you pile up homes and ask, "Why not
> push back that noisy strip of bay, that ocean
> bank that makes me feel less rich?")

The verses show psychological insight, if not charity. Nervous instability, "piling up" of homes, impatience at being hemmed in by the coastline—all this betrays a strong unconscious fear of death, which, like the sea, confines us all and cannot be made to retreat for very long. But private stupidity also creates a social problem that Horace recognizes as being extremely serious; for in his seemingly boundless expansion, the capitalist uproots little people from their homes.

With equal satiric vigor, Odes II, 15 contrasts the unproductive pleasure dwellings and gardens of contemporary millionaires with the good old days when Romans spent more in the public sector, on temples and municipal buildings.[10] And as, in Odes II, 18, greed and selfishness transgress religiously sanctioned boundaries, so in III, 24, civil wars will repeat themselves endlessly unless they are expiated by moral reform and at least a symbolic renunciation of private wealth. While these early odes moralize too much, they express a genuine sentiment: Horace's longing for social reforms, such as Octavian was beginning to propose, and his passionate sense of the necessity of regeneration if Rome is to survive. In this way, they link the satires of 41-31 B.C. with the "Roman Odes" of 27 B.C. That death or luxury, however, have any personal meaning to Horace, or that he too has experienced, let alone triumphed over, unconscious fears and desires is hardly evident from these "satiric odes."

A greater sympathy with other men, and a correspondingly more mature definition of the poet's own life, appears in Odes II, 16, which was written before the first Roman Ode.

> Otium divos rogat in patenti
> prensus Aegaeo, simul atra nubes
> condidit lunam neque certa fulgent
>   sidera nautis;
>
> otium bello furiosa Thrace,
> otium Medi pharetra decori,
> Grosphe, non gemmis neque purpura ve-
>   nale neque auro.
>
> non enim gazae neque consularis
> summovet lictor miseros tumultus
> mentis et curas laqueata circum
>   tecta volantis.
>
> vivitur parvo bene, cui paternum
> splendet in mensa tenui salinum
> nec levis somnos timor aut cupido
>   sordidus aufert.
>
> quid brevi fortes iaculamur aevo
> multa? quid terras alio calentis
> sole mutamus? patriae quis exsul
>   se quoque fugit?

scandit aeratas vitiosa navis
Cura nec turmas equitum relinquit,
ocior cervis et agente nimbos
    ocior Euro.

laetus in praesens animus quod ultra est
oderit curare et amara lento
temperet risu; nihil est ab omni
    parte beatum.

abstulit clarum cita mors Achillem,
longa Tithonum minuit senectus,
et mihi forsan, tibi quod negarit,
    porriget hora.

te greges centum Siculaeque circum
mugiunt vaccae, tibi tollit hinnitum
apta quadrigis equa, te bis Afro
    murice tinctae

vestiunt lanae; mihi parva rura et
spiritum Graiae tenuem Camenae
Parca non mendax dedit et malignum
    spernere vulgus.

(For peace the man trapped on the open
Aegean prays, when the moon is buried
in dark clouds and no star is gleaming
to guide the sailor home. For peace,
Thracians raging in war, for peace gay-
quivered Persians pray: no jewels pur-
chase it, Grosphus. Gold and purples
never do.

Bank accounts and bodyguards cannot dis-
perse the unhappy crowds of anxious
Cares. Under the gilded ceilings they
fly about. He lives nicely whose father's
salt cellar gleams on a plain
table; he rests easy. Fear and desire
cannot disturb his sleep.

Why bravely aim in our short lives at so
much? Why exchange our homes for lands
warmed by another sun? Can we outrun

ourselves? On brazen ships corrupting
Care climbs aboard; with cavalry squads
she rides apace, swifter than deer or
cloud-dispersing winds.

Minds that enjoy what's here refuse to
worry; bitterness they blend with a
slow smile. Nothing can be perfect on
every side. Famous Achilles swiftly died,
Tithonus lived to creep about. What time
denies you, it may lavish generously on me.

A hundred fine Sicilian herds moo for
your pleasure, brood mares neigh by your
chariot, wools twice-dipped in African
purple clothe your body. *My* income from
Fate is assured: the small country, the
subtle breath of the Greek Muse rising
above the crowd.)

The first four stanzas are half satiric. As Lucretius showed, men
strive for security in ways that betray them. They amass riches and
power when they ought instead to limit desire and fear. Horace
shows us from the beginning what neurotic anxiety feels like.
Through vowel contrast, clash of word accent and ictus, and word
placement, he creates an atmosphere of exposure and dread. We
have all felt "lost at sea." Nor does he ridicule, as he might, those
lords whose worries overwhelm them like a surging revolutionary
mob. He means us to understand their anguish, to sympathize
with them—as we do not sympathize with the capitalist caricatured
in Odes II, 18. Their plight nonetheless serves as a foil to the happiness enjoyed by the quiet man with the shining saltcellar.

This man could be Horace. If so, it is significant that the poet
returns, in stanza 5, to the usual struggle of life. Horace can instruct Grosphus and others because his heart, like theirs, is treacherous; he too has nourished far-flung hopes, has forgotten, or tried
to forget, life's shortness, has desired "lands warmed by another
sun" (an image which, like Eliot's "We go south in the winter,"
implies a systematic evasion of the knowledge of death). The
attempt is futile. It brings the greater nightmare of stanza 6. But
it is also deeply human. We saw earlier how Horace used self-

parody in Satires II, 6 and Epode 2 to acknowledge and surmount his own tendency to escapism. When Davus crudely psychoanalyzes him, in Satires II, 7, 111-15,

> " . . . adde quod idem
> non horam tecum esse potes, non otia recte
> ponere, teque ipsum vitas fugitivus et erro,
> iam vino quaerens, iam somno fallere curam:
> frustra; nam comes atra premit sequiturque
> fugacem."

> ("Item: you can't live with yourself one
> hour. You've no idea of leisure. You
> avoid yourself like a slave running away
> from master, drinking a lot, sleeping a
> lot, trying to fool old Care. No use:
> she's at your footsteps—she will catch you!")

his zeal affords comedy, but it also reflects Horace's real self-awareness and self-control. The poet is more than a parlor analyst. His insight into his own emotional experience gives him a constant, quick, and charitable awareness of the hidden motives by which other men are driven, the burden of unhappiness they carry, their lives of quiet or shrill desperation.

In Odes II, 16, as in the ode to Plancus, his "solution" to life's problems is neither impersonal nor absolute. Since anxiety is inherent in the human condition, it cannot be explained away like a neurosis; it is rather a "bitterness" in things, to be "blended," as we mix a drink, "with a slow smile." The realization that life is not "perfect on every side" could lead to cynicism, but rightly accepted (though with a certain wilfulness: Horace will "refuse to worry" and down his drink), it frees him to look on the brighter side of things. Achilles and Tithonus demanded everything—and got nothing. Horace asks little and gets much. That is one of Fate's ironies. If happiness resists being pursued, the accepting heart is sometimes surprised by joy. Horace is a poet, not an Epicurean; he bypasses tranquility in order to live, not more quietly, but more completely; and tranquility catches him up, as Care pursued those others: an unsolicited gift, accompanying, but not defining, the poet's existence.

[56]

III *Transcendence of Boundaries*

To gain what happiness open-eyed experience allows: that is the province Horace explored and conquered in Rome's name. Perhaps his temperament, sociable and solitary by turns, influenced his two-sided perception of the good life. To live sensibly and well, a man must respect nature's boundaries; but to understand other lives and live his own most fully, he must frequently overstep long-trusted, well-defined positions. Right growth depends on more than philosophical instruction. It requires courage, honesty, and faith.

Faith is not one of Horace's better-known qualities. Here again we must revert to the question of Virgil's influence on him, and to Virgil's idea of leisure, which, while it includes inner joy and openness to the world, implies a literary and moral imperative, of *moving forward.* The past must continually be left behind—in order, however, that the best of it may be preserved.

Further "shade" at the end of Eclogue 10 would "harm the crops." Virgil's mood is elegiac, like Spenser's in his *December.* He must "arise" and go, like the goats, so his life may bear fruit. A less personal, larger-scale advance is necessary in history, however much we may weep for the uncivilized beauty and happiness that must perish along with ancient wildness and evil. A modern trilogy, *The Lord of the Rings,* by J. R. R. Tolkien, tells the same story as the *Georgics* and the *Aeneid.* The old must be burned away. A hero may look back and weep, but he must move into the future.

Virgil defines Aeneas' forward movement in religious terms. Each step is marked by a dream or vision, prophetic of the future and revelatory of inner purpose. For religion, to Virgil, is not, as it was to Lucretius, a kind of bondage by which fear-driven men forfeit their rightful security and freedom. It is, rather, a faith that widens the human horizon and increases man's freedom even as it defines his responsibility. As for security, that is a false goal. In order to achieve the goal thrust upon him by Fate, Aeneas must give up premature attempts to settle down and "rebuild Troy," must risk himself at sea, in the underworld, and traveling up the Tiber, and, casting off his older identity as the snake sloughs its skin, must be spiritually reborn and initiated into the future.

There were, thought Virgil, more things in heaven and earth than were dreamed of in Epicurean philosophy (*Georgics* II, 490-94):

> felix qui potuit rerum cognoscere causas,
> atque metus omnis et inexorabile fatum
> subiecit pedibus strepitumque Acherontis avari.
> fortunatus et ille deos qui novit agrestis
> Panaque Silvanumque senem Nymphasque sorores.

> (Happy the man who found out nature's
> science, who trampled down inexorable
> fate and fear of death and rushing Acheron.
> Fortunate too, who knows the rural gods:
> Pan, old Silvanus, and the sister Nymphs.)

Lucretius' poetry was fruitful. Virgil praises him wholeheartedly, much as we praise "the great Jewish poet, Freud"[11] for the heroism with which he explored the psychic underworld, bringing liberation from neurotic fears. But while Lucretius and Freud tasted the joy that accompanies great invention, what they offered others was only negative, relief from mental pain. Psychoanalysis is often necessary to remove impediments to right growth, but often, too, it becomes an opiate, a means of avoiding responsibility. Virgil's acceptance of distress and toil, on the other hand, is matched by his power of receiving joy. For him, as for the hardworking countrymen, the rural gods are real presences, and joy springs up where they walk. Faith constitutes a demand and a risk, but also a promise. The Golden Age, which we thought had perished, will be restored. Rome will be built (though Aeneas will never see it), peace and joy will reign throughout the world.

Perhaps this vision came through the "ivory gate" of false dreams. What is remarkable, and a great tribute to Virgil, is that Horace incorporated so much of it into his life and poetry.[12] Thus Faunus, a tamer Pan, visits the Sabine farm, which is described in Golden Age traits in Odes III, 18 and I, 17 (lines 1-4):

> Velox amoenum saepe Lucretilem
> mutat Lycaeo Faunus et igneam
> defendit aestatem capellis
> usque meis pluviosque ventos.

> (Quickly Faunus leaves his Arcadian
> Mount to visit Lucretilis here:
> from fiery heat he preserves my goats
> and from stormy rains.)

Virgil's influence can be seen in the way in which Horace shares the feelings of his flock, and they his; in the transference of the Peaceable Kingdom from an imaginary fairyland in the West to a real Sabine farm; and in the centrality, emphasized by position, of a sense of religious dedication (lines 13-14) :

> di me tuentur, dis pietas mea
> et Musa cordi est.

> (The gods protect me, the gods cherish my reverence and Muse.)

At the same time, Horace's enthusiasm is qualified by reserved, self-critical humor.[13] We saw this earlier, in Epode 2. If Odes I, 17 begins as pastoral, it ends in a sophisticated flirtation, a dramatic situation worthy of Callimachus. Horace is a "professor of love" (*praeceptor amoris,* the Greek *erôtodidaskalos*), and his offer to Tyndaris, a local "Helen of Troy," of asylum from the destructive passions of the city is surely less innocent than it appears. While the playful erotic element, like the satirical ending of Epode 2, hardly affects the seriousness with which Horace proclaims his enjoyment of the country, it brings it down to earth in a way that even Virgil's thorns in the ankle and rutting he-goats never do. We are, in the end, among people, not gods or animals. Moreover, Horace's insistence on security is un-Virgilian. The principal grace of the Sabine farm is its solitary location in a beautiful withdrawn valley, *in reducta valle.* The phrase is repeated from Epode 2, where Horace-Alfius invoked Silvanus, symbolically, as *tutor finium,* "protector of bounds," and destined a lamb to be slain on the *Terminalia,* or Feast of Boundaries. It is a good life, well shaded and well defined, and Horace has little desire, or reason, to abandon it.

Here, indeed, Horace parts company with Virgil. If the *pietas,* or reverence, of Aeneas forces him again and again to abandon security, Horace's *pietas* implies no such heroic commitment; and although the bounds within which he "may safely graze" are spiritual, they still remain, familiar, reliable, and protective. So much for himself; but what of his dear friend? Odes I, 3, a bon voyage poem to Virgil as he takes ship for Greece, surprises us with its passion; good wishes and banter quickly give way to a gloomy meditation on the rashness of heroic daring and—rising to a final denunciation—the overwhelming power of sin:

> nil mortalibus ardui est:
> caelum ipsum petimus stultitia neque
>   per nostrum patimur scelus
>   iracunda Iovem ponere fulmina.

> (Nothing is hard for mortals: like fools we
> storm Heaven itself; our sins make Jove unable
>   to lay his angry lightning down.)

Although Horace consciously exaggerates his own feelings, the poem cannot have been intended simply to amuse Virgil. It shows that Horace has thought long and hard about the *Aeneid*, begun perhaps three years before, and it continues the unending argument between the two friends that began with the interchange of Epode 16 and Eclogue 4. Of course, Horace was genuinely worried about Virgil's physical safety. Sea trips were dangerous, and the Romans had less confidence in ships than we have today in airplanes. But more: Virgil's view of *pietas* perhaps seemed to be exposing him, as it did his hero, to spiritual risk and suffering. Like Aeneas, he was stepping out in faith, in a way that common sense judged to be absurd. It is a fearful thing to see a friend, especially one who is "half of my soul," leave the bounds of safety.

Seen against this background, Horace's reorientation of mind in the so-called "conversion ode," I, 34, is all the more remarkable.

> Parcus deorum cultor et infrequens
> insanientis dum sapientiae
>   consultus erro, nunc retrorsum
>   vela dare atque iterare cursus

> cogor relictos; namque Diespiter,
> igni corusco nubila dividens
>   plerumque, per purum tonantis
>   egit equos volucremque currum,

quo bruta tellus et vaga flumina,
quo Styx et invisi horrida Taenari
   sedes Atlanteusque finis
     concutitur. valet ima summis

mutare et insignem attenuat deus,
obscura promens; hinc apicem rapax
   fortuna cum stridore acuto
     sustulit, hic posuisse gaudet.

(Sparing in worship once, when I took a wrong
philosophical direction, I must now turn and sail
out to sea again: for Jove, who ordinarily hurls
his lightning in cloudy skies, has driven his
team and thundering chariot through the blue,
and struck! The heavy earth, its running streams,
Styx, underworld, and the bounds of Atlas—all
were shaken! God can change high for low, humble
the proud and bring to light the obscure, as
Fortune whirls off one man's crown, joyfully, for
another.)

The idea of conversion is misleading, since Horace neither turns
nor returns to any definite religious or philosophical belief. He
pretends, but only ironically, to carry out the prediction of Lucretius, that amazement at some natural phenomenon would eventually compel his readers to "backslide" into the irrational domain
of religion (V, 82-90):

nam bene qui didicere deos securum agere aevum,
si tamen interea mirantur qua ratione
quaeque geri possint, praesertim rebus in illis
quae supera caput aetheriis cernuntur in oris,
rursus in antiquas referuntur religiones
et dominos acris adsciscunt, omnia posse
quos miseri credunt, ignari quid queat esse,
quid nequeat, finita potestas denique cuique
quanam sit ratione atque alte terminus haerens.

(Those even who have learned how the gods
lead untroubled lives are sometimes forced
to wonder just how things happen [which is
especially true of things high overhead in

the airy regions]: swiftly they slip back
into old beliefs, and recognize grim over-
lords, who can [they think] do anything—
not knowing what is possible, what not, the
limit fixed for every force, the deep-set
boundary mark.)

If Horace had really rejoined the Church, it would be doubly
ironic: for not only did he once refuse, echoing Lucretius, to be
impressed by a pretended miracle in a small town in southern
Italy (Satires I, 5, 101),

namque deos didici securum agere aevum; . . .

(for I have learned how the gods lead
untroubled lives; . . .)

but Epicurus taught, not that thunderbolts could never fall from
a clear sky, but that all phenomena are capable of *some* scientific
explanation, even if this cannot immediately be ascertained.

Horace is not reconverted like the fool in Lucretius to some
earlier belief. He never "went to church" much in the first place.
But neither is Odes I, 34 merely the self-ironical representation of
a transient mood of religious awe (leading to a fairly conventional
meditation on fortune). Critics have been led into the one error
or, by reaction, into the other, by their misunderstanding of Horace's sailing metaphor. For *vela dare atque iterare cursus relictos*
does not mean to retrace a particular course, which once was
abandoned, but to set out again on the sea, like Teucer in Odes I, 7,

cras ingens iterabimus aequor,

or like Aeneas, who is compelled by uncanny phenomena to abandon false positions of security and venture anew into the unknown
(*Aeneid* III, 190-91):

hanc quoque deserimus sedem paucisque relictis
vela damus vastumque cava trabe currimus aequor.

(This resting place too we forsake. A few
are left behind. We give sail, and our ships
run swiftly over the vast plain of the sea.)

[62]

Virgil's metaphors, as ever, are far from dead. Aeneas "gives" not only sail but self to the race (*currimus*, cf. Horace's *cursus*) over the uncharted sea. To fulfill his destiny, he must pluck up premature roots (*deserimus*) and sacrifice the happiness of prolonging security and repose. This theme is recurrent in the *Aeneid*. Horace too has courage; only, unlike Aeneas, he must risk insecurity without the promise (however gradually revealed) of a final resting place and goal. As he says later, in Epistles I, 1, "Where the storm sweeps me away, there I pay my respects."

In Odes I, 34, the sailing metaphor is combined with another, the "shaking of the bounds," which describes both the external phenomenon and Horace's inner reaction. Reality, emotion, reflection are interwoven here. While *concutitur* recalls the repeated warning of Lucretius, that man's instinctive terror at some surprising act of nature may hurl him back, helpless, into religious bondage, the point of *finis concutitur* quite reverses Lucretius' teaching. For Horace's reaction to the thunderbolt is more than an emotional reflex. The event heightens his awareness of the real nature of the universe, which is mirrored in his subjective response. When Lucretius rejected the possibility of divine intervention in human life, he relied on a basic, often stated theorem: the fixed limit in nature, "the deep-set boundary mark." His whole poem, in fact, revolves around the twin concepts of limit and law: the natural boundaries of creation and destruction, and the corresponding ethical limits, or limitations of desire and fear, in which the Epicurean convert must acquiesce if he is to attain true peace of mind. But what if the bounds to which Lucretius finally appealed could be shaken, as for Horace they are? (Or what, if our mathematics are no longer Euclidian, or our physics Newtonian?) A comfortable position of skeptical rationalism cannot be adequate either to the scientist's investigations or to the poet's awareness of reality. That is why Horace is carried out to sea; why he resigns the "untroubled life" (*securum aevum*) of Epicurean gods and (perhaps) men; and why he acknowledges an irrational force governing human life—the very consequence that Lucretius feared, as an intolerable threat to human security. To Horace, Fortuna is at once less impersonal than the "blind chance" to whose power Epicurus set limits and less responsible than the goddess whom the Stoics identified with Jupiter, Providence, and Fate. She restores no moral balance, only plays at hazard with crowns and lives.

To claim, then, as Horace did in I, 26, to be set apart from cares, is to occupy an untenable position. Care is inherent in the world. Mental barriers simply will not hold. If Horace could appeal to nature's limits, in Odes I, 7, to alleviate Plancus' anxiety, he must with equal fidelity to nature renounce those limits of security that, in Odes I, 34, are so dramatically pronounced inadequate. Fortune may still be defeated, and anxiety overcome, as the great ode, III, 29, will show. They must, however, be confronted on open ground: or, in Horace's metaphor, open sea.

But if the last word of Odes I, 34 counts, Horace's dominant feeling may be, not irony nor regret, but a joyful sense of adventure. And further: although the modern equivalent of his "conversion" would be a departure, like that of Joyce, from traditional religious belief, his feeling (like Joyce's) is undeniably religious. A good analogue is Wordsworth's well-known experience, of rowing on a lake.[14]

> "... when from behind that craggy steep till then
> the horizon's bound, a huge peak, black and huge,
> as if with voluntary power instinct,
> upreared its head. . . ."

Although Wordsworth returned to shore, the experience impressed upon him a deep sense of sin and wonder. There is every reason to believe that Horace's experience was equally impressive. Italian storms *can be* sudden and terrifying. But while Wordsworth represents the occurrence, like Nature's other "severer interventions," as one element in a progressive and fairly uniform spiritual education, Odes I, 34 remains one lyric among many, as if to emphasize that no one experience or attitude should rightly dominate the rest. His collection stresses variety, not continuity; contrast, not chronology. All the same, critical study of Odes I, 34 and other odes discovers a courage, a continuing responsiveness to life, and a capacity to endure inner change and growth, that quite match the corresponding faculties in Wordsworth.

IV *Renewal of Spirit*

Although none of the odes so far discussed has any monopoly on Horace's thought or shapes any definitive answer to his problems, taken together they show the difference between his Golden Mean and the abstract moral cliché it has since become. Not only must we (as Horace recommends in Odes II, 10) steer a middle course, neither sailing too far to sea nor hugging the rocky shore: as we grow older, the terms of life's voyage are constantly changing. Horace's maturity consists largely in his willingness to acknowledge and accept this change. And this responsiveness, heightened by a sense of poetic vocation, in turn affects his conception of lyric poetry: for to "represent" Alcaeus in Rome required a reorientation of mind like that of Odes I, 34, and the passing of a previously determined limit.

This second conversion appears in Odes III, 25, to Bacchus. Here, as in I, 34, Horace is excited into a condition of heightened awareness, which he joyfully welcomes: "sweet is the risk" (the oxymoron marks his abandonment again of the calculus of security). But Odes III, 25 is directed less than I, 34 to the nature of reality, and more to a fresh and vigorous artistic power in the poet, which is mirrored in a headlong, dithyrambic rhythm (contrast the more restrained ode to Virgil, in the same meter), and in metaphors of intoxication, transported vision, and even insanity:

> Quo me, Bacche, rapis tui
> plenum? quae nemora aut quos agor in specus
>   velox mente nova? quibus
> antris egregii Caesaris audiar
>   aeternum meditans decus
> stellis inserere et consilio Iovis?
>   dicam insigne recens adhuc
> indictum ore alio. non secus in iugis
>   exsomnis stupet Euhias
> Hebrum prospiciens et nive candidam
>   Thracen ac pede barbaro
> lustratam Rhodopen, ut mihi devio
>   ripas et vacuum nemus
> mirari libet. o Naiadum potens
>   Baccharumque valentium

proceras manibus vertere fraxinos,
    nil parvum aut humili modo,
nil mortale loquar. dulce periculum est,
    o Lenaee, sequi deum
cingentem viridi tempora pampino.

(Bacchus, where do you rush your votary
away? What groves or caves await a mind
renewed? Where shall my voice be heard,
practicing to raise Caesar's lasting
glory to Jove's councils? My
song will be splendid, fresh, unheard-
of before: as, amazed, the sleepless
Bacchante stands and stares at the wilder-
ness of snowy Thrace—its frozen
rivers and danced-on peaks: so *I* love
leaving the road, to gaze on river banks
and deserted groves. O Master, who can
make women's hands overturn ash trees:
no little, creeping song that perishes
I'll sing! Sweet his risk who follows
the god binding his head with the crown
of vine leaves.[15])

Although Horace is "full of Bacchus," he is not merely drunk and "seeing things."[16] Openness to life's wonder demands greater courage, and produces a finer intoxication, than common wine-bibbers know.

In his symbolic removal from normal haunts and everyday behavior, Horace recaptures the prophetic self-assurance of the "inspired" classical poet. He may therefore address *egregius Caesar* on reasonably equal terms;[17] and in the Roman Odes, he will. Yet the present ode is more than a prelude to specific political poems. Instead, the particular change of mind (*mente nova*) by which Horace feels empowered to sing of Caesar, even promise him apotheosis, is only one facet of a larger renewal of spirit. Horace hints as much when he extends familiar metaphors beyond their customary significance. The adjective, *devio*, implies Hellenistic refinement of technique and originality of subject matter: "At all costs," Callimachus taught, "avoid the high-road of song." But once "by-pathology" is exhausted, the creative poet may regain the highway with splendid originality. Again, *vacuum nemus* suggests Hellenistic isolation. Horace used *vacuus* in Odes I, 6 of his emotionally uninvolved life and writing. But if the cool, empty grove of III, 25 is, like poetry itself, a retreat, it is no less a place of initiation, like the groves from which Aeneas heroically emerges in Aeneid VI and VIII.[18] It is as though Horace's retreat into himself—his full enjoyment of *otium*—generated an outward movement strong enough to crack an earlier poetic and philosophic shell. If, elsewhere, Apollo is invoked to guarantee the continuance of his "subtle" and secure poetic life, Bacchus is a fitting symbol of the creative force that transcends Hellenistic limit (*nil parvum aut humili modo*) while yet fulfilling the most stringent Hellenistic requirements of poetic originality and force.

If one aspect of Horace's "renewal of spirit" is the desire to write political poetry, its corollary is his altered relationship with Alcaeus, shown in Odes I, 32.

> Poscimur. si quid vacui sub umbra
> lusimus tecum, quod et hunc in annum
> vivat et pluris, age dic Latinum,
>   barbite, carmen,
>
> Lesbio primum modulate civi,
> qui ferox bello, tamen inter arma
> sive iactatam religarat udo
>   litore navim,
>
> Liberum et Musas Veneremque et illi
> semper haerentem puerum canebat
> et Lycum nigris oculis nigroque
>   crine decorum.
>
> o decus Phoebi et dapibus supremi
> grata testudo Iovis, o laborum
> dulce lenimen, mihi cumque salve
>   rite vocanti.
>
> (They call. If quietly we played, under
> the trees, tunes to endure this year
> and longer, grant me a Roman song, dear
> lyre: your strings were first attuned by
> a man from Lesbos, a fierce fighter, who
> sometimes rested, laying his weapons down

or tying his ship to the damp shore: of
Bacchus then he would sing, the Muses,
Venus, close-embraced by her son, and
Lycus, whose black hair and black eyes
so gracefully became him. O tortoise
shell, you who grace the hands of Apollo
and feasts of highest Jove, sweet
refreshment of labor, hear me when I
call unto you.)

In the ode to Agrippa, Horace restricted his lyre to "peaceful"
themes, drinking and lovemaking. He now justifies the request
of a "Roman song" by invoking the precedent of Alcaeus, a "citizen" (*civis,* Greek *politês*) whose lyric verse spanned public and
private life, or better, knew no distinction between the two. Nothing could be more surprising than Horace's saying "Yes!" (if
we read *poscimur*) to a request, probably from Maecenas, that he
write about Roman themes. Nothing, too, could better indicate
his newfound confidence and freedom.

Hope though we may, with Professor Fraenkel, that the ghosts
of *Orazio maggiore e minore* are well laid,[19] we must nevertheless
realize that Horace often flirts with the idea of divorcing private
life from public concern (see Epode 16, and Odes I, 6 and II, 1, to
Agrippa and Pollio). In the present ode, the dichotomy is suggested but then transcended. By a superficial view, Alcaeus' lyric
poetry was an interlude (*inter arma*) between more weighty
concerns. Yet Horace not only indicates, by a syntactical ambiguity,[20] that both kinds of poetry, "playful" and "Roman," are
valuable and will endure: by sound- and word-repetition, and by
the summarizing epithet,

o laborum/dulce lenimen,

he shows us that whatever greatness the lyre may achieve is derived
from its single power to refresh and renew our spirits. The idea is
Pindaric; and as we shall see in the Pindarizing ode, III, 4, Horace's political poetry, far from being versified politics, embodies
the poet's desire to extend personal renewal to society, his wish—
whether practical or not—to embrace private and public welfare
in a unifying harmony.

If we are surprised that a poet who cherished solitude as much as Horace did should come so emphatically to deny the separateness of his private world, we should remember once more that Virgil led the way. The *Aeneid* and the Roman Odes grow in the same, organic way from Hellenistic privacy and shade to their full Roman and classical fruition. Far from cutting themselves off from their roots when they write political poetry, Virgil and Horace achieve a new rootedness, whose outward manifestation is their return to classical models. It may be that a modern poet can no more overcome the Hellenistic division once and for all than he can return to the womb; but he can still be reborn, like Aeneas, into his spiritual inheritance. And if the conflict between the worlds, ever threatening to diverge, provides a continual excitement in Horace's poetry, as in Virgil's, the sense of wholeness that both poets radiate, resting as it does on their endurance of personal and literary tensions, constitutes a great part of their claim to immortality.

CHAPTER 4

The Roman Odes[1]

I *Sincerity*

WITH typical heavy-handed humor, Augustus once asked Horace to address an epistle to him: "Or are you afraid that your reputation with posterity will suffer if it appears that you were my friend?"[2] Precisely, Horace's reputation has suffered and still suffers. In his political poems, on which, as Fraenkel says, his reputation as a lyric poet must largely depend,[3] he seems to many critics to assume an alien, uncomfortable role; for, to put it bluntly, how could a sensitive and honest poet praise Augustus?

As the attack on Horace's "sincerity" becomes more sophisticated, refutation becomes harder but more important. Nobody today charges Virgil or Horace with outright propaganda. Although our view of Augustus is still partially distorted by the twentieth-century experience of fascism and especially Mussolini's cheap brand of *Romanitá,* we no longer see Maecenas as a minister of propaganda or the poets as hired broadcasters. In proof of their honesty, it has been noted that Propertius jeered at Augustus' marriage laws; that Virgil's poems reflect dispossession, cruelty, and suffering, as well as the new peace and prosperity; and that Horace not only often refused to write panegyrical effusions on demand, but even declined a position as Augustus' private secretary. Like Virgil, too (to anticipate), he always qualified praise of Augustus with admonitions of how it must be earned. The problem remains. Octavian-Augustus was a cold, calculating, enigmatic figure, an actor and politician, who fought ruthlessly for an absolute power which he then wielded with discretion and sense, and who, unlike Julius Caesar, sufficiently valued the political forms and religious-moral ideals of the republic to preserve or restore these where he could. Historians give him credit for behaving more decently after Actium (though decency can be self-interested) than most would have prophesied, and for bestowing on the Senate and the Roman people not only peace and order, which were absolutely necessary, but a far greater share of freedom and dignity than his successors allowed (few people wished to return to the "liberty," bloodshed, and chaos of the late republic). Perhaps Augustus may even be conceded a share in the virtues, *fortitudo, clementia, iustitia,* and *pietas,* for which the senate awarded him a golden shield in 27. We must still ask: could this play actor and politician inspire real poetry? Granted that the Roman Odes were not written to order: but was "Horace's heart in them"?

Whether these are good poems, each reader must decide for himself. To me, they are; but my immediate concern is with the problem of the heart raised by Wilkinson and La Penna, among others.[4] How did Horace relate himself to Augustus and Rome?

In Odes I, 14, he accepted emotional involvement with the Ship of State, as a lover accepts the suffering that true love entails (lines 17-18):

> nuper sollicitum quae mihi taedium,
> nunc desiderium curaque non levis.

At the same time, Odes I, 14 shows his other tendency, to withdrawal; for unlike Alcaeus, he represents himself not as aboard the storm-battered ship, but watching it from shore.[5] Indeed, the safe harbor into which he urges it to sail may stand on a personal level for the withdrawn, Epicurean life. The realm of politics *was* uncomfortable and alien to Horace. His commitment to Rome, which accords with his personal development discussed earlier ("following the god"), shows itself most characteristically in his endurance of a tension between political concern and the desire to escape into a safer, happier, more private world.

The ideals, however, of simplicity and restraint for which Horace pleads in the Roman Odes are not alien but rest on his personal experience. The "social odes" (II, 18; II, 15; III, 24) make an obvious bridge from Sabine contentment to Roman politics. But could Horace really have believed after Actium that Augustus would effect a regeneration of the Roman spirit? To suggest that Virgil thought so begs the question. A certain optimism, if not enthusiasm, was conceivable in 29-27 B.C. Octavian rebuilt temples

and experimented with marriage laws; above all, he declined un-
traditional titles and forms of rule. Not only did he shun Julius
Caesar's monarchical affectations: he seemed bent on the far-rang-
ing reforms that Cicero had recommended in 46 B.C. as a last chance
to save the Republic and Caesar's life.[6] Caesar ignored the advice, reformed little but the calendar, and was shortly assassinated.
The restoration of 27 B.C. held better promise. Octavian's decision
to become Augustus, not a second Romulus, seemed prophetic:
like Aeneas, he was turned in the right direction. Why, then,
should a virtuous, happy, and even golden age not begin anew?

In retrospect, we are disappointed. So, probably, were Virgil
and Horace. The ideals they held up to Augustus and Rome out-
stripped the intentions or the ability of either. It is ironic that,
while Horace appealed romantically to the Romans to jettison
riches, Augustus was prudently encouraging industry, commerce,
and capitalism;[7] and while Horace demanded a Parthian War to
wipe the bloodstains of civil war off Roman swords, Augustus was
delaying and preparing eventually to negotiate a sound Parthian
peace. Yet Horace was no fool. He never forgot for long that politics is the art of the possible. That is why, although, like Virgil,
he looks to Augustus as a savior, prays fervently for his success, encourages his efforts, and even awards him conditional semidivine
honors, his aspirations (perhaps also like Virgil's) are generally
accompanied by an equal pessimism, a feeling that the old Roman
virtues cannot be restored, that the downward pull of history is
too strong.

In the Roman Odes, therefore, he explores a deeply poetic subject: the contrast between the darkness of the recent Roman past,
with its almost unbroken chain of civil wars caused by selfishness
and greed, and the brightness of a simpler, better Roman ideal
that shines out of the legendary past and may or may not be recre-
ated. While this contrast dramatizes the urgency of a dramatic
break with late republican corruption, it also reflects Horace's
awareness that genuine moral reform, and so lasting peace, was
unlikely. But if so, should not a sensitive poet remove himself
from Roman troubles, to the islands or harbor or garden of private
imagining? Regression is always attractive. Hence the poetic intensity of the Roman Odes, their dramatic excitement as a group,
and—if the word still means anything—their sincerity.

II *Contemplation of History*

The first two stanzas of Odes III, 1, which introduce the cycle, include complementary but clashing themes.

> Odi profanum vulgus et arceo;
> favete linguis: carmina non prius
>   audita Musarum sacerdos
>   virginibus puerisque canto.
>
> regum timendorum in proprios greges,
> reges in ipsos imperium est Iovis,
>   clari Giganteo triumpho,
>   cuncta supercilio moventis.

> (Hence, you uninitiated! Silence for the
> Muses' priest, who brings to youths
> and maidens songs never before presented!
> Kings govern their flocks with fear, kings
> themselves are governed by Jove, who defeat-
> ed the Giants, nods an eyebrow and sways
> the world.)

These verses are grave, ceremonious. Sacred rites are beginning, pay heed, reverence god-given power! But whereas in stanza 1 Horace insists on privacy and the specialness of poet and audience alike, rejecting the gross public, stanza 2 subjects the individual to menacing, uncontrollable forces. Jove's all-shaking eyebrow, like his thunderbolt, symbolizes less a rational order in the world than an irrational violence. That is what history feels like. It is a long step from bucolic to epic, from Faunus and the goats to Jove and his flock of kings.

Like its proem, Odes III, 1 may be read two ways. Its argument is basically Epicurean. If death levels all ranks, and riches and power fail to dispel fears, but the poor countryman is happier, why should Horace build extravagantly? From later odes the chain of propositions acquires political relevance. Sabine frugality and restraint are the only sure basis of national regeneration. Yet somehow, the ending is too personal:

> cur valle permutem Sabina
>   divitias operosiores?

> (Why change my Sabine valley for
> more burdensome revenue?)

The dissonance was planned. While Horace apparently stresses the power of necessity, especially that of death, to convince his audience that riches and power are inadequate and treacherous goals (much as he showed in II, 16 that men's usual ways of striving for security increase and do not alleviate their anxiety), the ode itself shows a dramatic movement away from anxiety, whether personal, historical , or cosmic, and its ending is as much a recoil from Roman concern as an implicit recommendation of a Roman virtue. The Sabine farm is not only an example but an escape.

Nor is the dissonance between public necessity and private happiness altogether resolved in Odes III, 2. Here Horace demonstrates how simplicity of life benefits society. The youth who learns to "live on good terms with narrow poverty" will fight well, avenge Parthian insults, and expiate the civil wars—an abiding wish of Horace. Yet his famous statement, that "Death for the fatherland is sweet and proper," (line 13),

> dulce et decorum est pro patria mori,

seems paradoxical and forced. "Proper," yes; why "sweet"? Although Horace reinforces the point with a more private corollary, that we cannot outrun death, and although the picture of the dying patriot at least elicits more sympathy than the Homeric comparison of the victorious Roman soldier to a ravening lion, we are relieved when Horace, perhaps following an ode of Simonides, passes from military valor to a more generalized heroism that may be realized in peace, as in war, and even in the quiet, withdrawn life of a loyal citizen.

Hero and poet share the inner resolution that defies the mob; and the latter, who serves less conspicuously, is entitled like the soldier and the general to a definite reward (lines 25-26):

> est et fideli tuta silentio
> merces.

> (Loyal silence also receives sure recompense.)

The verse, from Simonides, was a favorite of Augustus: appropriately so, for he needed loyalty more than valor. But *tuta* also implies the unheroic security of Horace's existence. The ending, again, is equivocal: an achieved reconciliation of private happiness and public responsibility, but also a flight from harsh public necessities like war and sacrifice into a more peaceful world.

Odes III, 3 pursues the image of the independent-minded hero (lines 1-8):

> Iustum et tenacem propositi virum
> non civium ardor prava iubentium,
>   non vultus instantis tyranni
>   mente quatit solida neque Auster,
>
> dux inquieti turbidus Hadriae,
> nec fulminantis magna manus Iovis:
>   si fractus illabatur orbis,
>   impavidum ferient ruinae.
>
> (The just man holds to his purpose. The mob's
> frenzied appeal, the tyrant's countenance,
> can never alter his resolution, or winds
> stirring the Adriatic, or great Jove
> brandishing thunder! Ruins of an exploded
> world could strike him, and he'd not fear.)

"By this art," Horace continues, many heroes won apotheosis, and so will Augustus, as Juno once accepted his forerunner, Quirinus (Romulus), and promised eternal greatness to the Roman people, on one condition (lines 58-60):

>   ne nimium pii
> rebusque fidentes avitae
>   tecta velint reparare Troiae.
>
> (Over-great loyalty must not dare
> to rebuild the fallen roofs of ancestral
> Troy.)

The thought is complicated. Its brunt falls on Juno's speech. Evidently, Augustus (and Rome with him) is to demonstrate heroic steadfastness and merit divine favor by an act of renunciation: but what is meant by rebuilding "ancestral Troy"?

Scholars have risen greedily to the bait of allegory. Troy must stand for Caesarism—or Eastern immorality—or irreligiosity—or the greed and anarchy of the late republic. To a degree, all these interpretations are correct. Where each goes wrong is in its exclusiveness, which reduces Horace's broad symbolism to a narrow one-to-one correspondence. We would do better to reflect on Aeneid II, which was perhaps completed by 27 B.C.; for Horace's ode pays tribute to Virgil and comments on his poem.

For Horace, as for Virgil, Troy represents much more than any specific social or political fault. No doubt, the *iustus vir*, like Aeneas, is an exemplar for Augustus and the Roman people, who in different ways must break with their past. Sin takes many shapes, mob rule and despotism are twin evils, and the ode's opening verses may imply both that Augustus rightly shuns Hellenistic or Caesarian pretensions and that the Roman people must guard against a resurgence of late republican disorder. More generally, however, Augustus and the Roman people must *look to the future*. It is hard to abandon the past. The ending of any age or civilization evokes tears: *sunt lacrimae rerum*. But as Aeneas displays *pietas* by leaving Troy, not dying for it, despite Priam's death and Hecuba's suffering; and as, again, he leaves Dido at Carthage, rejecting her Catullan demand of absolute personal loyalty—a more limited *pietas*—in order to fulfill a deeper responsibility, so Augustus and Rome must not postpone the claims of the future to any misguided reverence for the past (*nimium pii*). The decision to look forward is necessary and right. It is also very sad.

Although, then, Odes III, 3 concludes the account of self-discipline begun in III, 1 and carried through III, 2, it should not be read simply as a political recommendation. History, as Virgil realized, is shot through with tragedy even when our country and allies are most successful. Not only does the rise of one nation require, by isonomic compensation, the decline of another, but personal freedom must bend to historical necessity, the "man" to the "arms." How deeply the tragic nature of history impressed Horace may be seen, characteristically, in his abrupt ending:

> non hoc iocosae conveniet lyrae:
> quo, Musa, tendis? desine pervicax
> referre sermones deorum et
> magna modis tenuare parvis.

> (This will not fit the laughing lyre.
> My Muse, why so ambitious? Stop re-
> porting gods' conversation, strait'-
> ning great things in small compass.)

The recall of the Muse is a tribute to Virgil and a sincere admission that the themes raised in Odes III, 3 cannot adequately be treated in lyric verse. It also shows emotional distress, even rebellion, against the *pietas* just demanded. Prolonged contemplation of history is intolerable: better the world of love, laughter, and wine! It is as though the knot of tension that gradually builds up in Odes III, 1-3 has been, not resolved, but violently and arbitrarily cut.

III   *Renewal of Spirit*

If Odes III, 3 recalls the tragic second book of the *Aeneid*, Odes III, 4 returns to the idea of a world order symbolized in Aeneid I by Neptune's quelling of the storm. Horace is also indebted to Pindar,[8] but with a difference. In the First Pythian Ode, the *symphônia* of the lyre at once embraces Pindar's joyful creativity, the victory celebration for Hieron, the harmoniousness of a city state regulated in the "Doric mode," and the world rule of Olympian gods. Almost effortlessly, the three spheres, personal, political, and cosmic, are interrelated and unified through shifting metaphors of music, order, and control. For reasons suggested earlier, this unification of experience was more difficult for Horace. The slow, outward movement toward historical reality in Odes III, 1-3 creates an equal and opposite reaction, toward privacy (*non hoc conveniet*: literally, "this won't fit"). To reverse the process, bridge anew the gap between individual and state, and return to Pindar's vision of unity, Horace must turn inward and review his own development. This he does in Odes III, 4.

Slowly, insistently, with evident happiness, he describes how the Muses always protected him and always will. Only after nine stanzas does he mention Augustus, whom the same Muses refresh and counsel (lines 37-42):

> vos Caesarem altum, militia simul
> fessas cohortis abdidit oppidis,
>   finire quaerentem labores
>   Pierio recreatis antro.

vos lene consilium et datis et dato
gaudetis almae.

(When great Caesar hid away his weary
armies, seeking to end his labors,
he was refreshed within your Pierian
cave; for you carry gentle counsel
and rejoice at its acceptance.)

Although scholarly discussion has been lured, here too, by allegory, there is, thanks perhaps to the Muses, more agreement about this "gentle counsel" than about "Troy." As the gigantomachy myth narrated in the second half of the ode represents the continuing triumph of civilization over barbarism, reflected in recent history at Actium (as, for Pindar, it was at Himera), it also points a warning, that only humane behavior can save the victor from succumbing in his turn to the fate of the violent, self-destructive Giants who warred against the gods. Horace is being realistic. He knows that Augustus' rule was won and must be maintained by power, by armies never conclusively "hidden away" in the Italian towns. He also knows that Augustus must rule by a moral authority that depends not on brute force but on receptivity to the Muses' advice: to the principles, never outmoded, of political harmony.

Yet we should not dwell too exclusively on *lene consilium*. The preceding nine stanzas do more than "present the poet's credentials." They reaffirm the integrity of his imaginative life. Hence the deliberateness with which he places the Muses, as he and Virgil elsewhere place the *dei agrestes*, in a real Italic landscape and the day-to-day life of men,[9] and emphasizes once more the experience of "going beyond the bounds" (lines 9-13):

me fabulosae Vulture in Apulo
nutricis extra limina Pulliae
 ludo fatigatumque somno
  fronde nova puerum palumbes

texere. . . .

(Once I wandered Apulus' slopes beyond
the bounds my nurse set me, and weary
of playing, slept; so doves of faerie
covered me with fresh leaves. . . .)

Diction and mood recall the fairy-tale ode, I, 22. There, a wolf ran from the sacred lover, or poet. Now he restates his confidence that, with the Muses, he may explore far-flung, dangerous places, always unharmed (*inviolatus*). Just so, the imaginative journey from the Sabine farm to Rome—and all that Rome stands for—may be risked without loss of integrity.

At its deepest level, the ode is about renewal. When Augustus listens "in the Pierian cave" to Virgil reading from the *Georgics*,[10] he is more than refreshed, he is re-created. For as genuine leisure not only rests our bodies and minds for continued labor but restores us in spirit, so that the meaning and direction of our labor are transformed, so Octavian has been and is being changed into a wise and moderate ruler. Only by re-finding himself can he accomplish a second foundation of Rome. His model is Apollo, who never puts the bow from his shoulder—never, that is, relinquishes his power—but who gives himself to peace and harmony, bathing his locks in the Castalian spring. So his statue stands with bow and lyre before the poets' new home, the Palatine temple dedicated in 28 B.C. But not only Augustus and Apollo can relax and, in that attitude, symbolize and guarantee the continuance of civilized order. Horace too has been refreshed, like a runner getting his second wind. We saw his weariness at the end of Odes III, 3, where, like Octavian (but in another sense), he wished to "set bounds" to his labor. That ending was a regression; but regression, as some psychologists assert, is an essential factor in human development. Perhaps poets, like children, must retreat two steps in order to advance five. As the "inspired baby" Horace is described as enjoying a holy sleep, covered with new leaves (*fronde nova*; compare *mente nova* in III, 25), so the grown poet enjoys the god-given freshening of the spirit by which new self-understanding is won together with the strength to begin again. In this way, the hoped-for reformation of the Augustan age, which is the major theme of the Roman Odes, is intimately bound up with the personal renewal of spirit that leads the poet to write and continue to write these very poems; and the harmony he celebrates is not just in the world, but in himself, binding him to the world, and effecting an integrity of life that is most truly Pindaric and Virgilian.

IV *Ideal and Reality*

The reconciling power of the Muses makes Horace's plea for Roman and even Augustan reforms into poetry. Witness the ending of Odes III, 5, where military toughmindedness is exemplified in the martyrdom of Regulus (lines 49-56):

> atqui sciebat quae sibi barbarus
> tortor pararet; non aliter tamen
> dimovit obstantis propinquos
> et populum reditus morantem
>
> quam si clientum longa negotia
> diiudicata lite relinqueret,
> tendens Venafranos in agros
> aut Lacedaemonium Tarentum.

> (He knew what torture awaited him at
> savage Carthage, but nonetheless
> he shouldered aside kinsmen and
> folk delaying his return, as though,
> having resolved some long legal case,
> he were setting forth into Venafran
> country, or down to Spartan-born
> Tarentum.)

By this ending, one critic argued, "unbearable thoughts are diverted ... into less painful trivialities."[11] Elsewhere, yes; not here. We should feel, as Horace did, the inner connection between Regulus' stern resolution to return to Carthage, where he would be tortured and killed, and the quiet happiness of the lawyer setting forth, his affairs finally wound up, for a country holiday. In both cases, the ordinary complication of life is resolved by a simple and proper act. The final image, *Lacedaemonium Tarentum*, suggests how love of the world's beauty is akin to love of the beauty of "Spartan" self-denial.[12]

The same nostalgia for *simplification of life* may be felt in Odes III, 6, where the closeness of Horace's plea, for a return to ancestral piety and chastity, to Augustus' actual religious and social program has incurred the charge of rhetoric, if not propaganda. We remember with a smile how Augustus lectured the Senate fathers on old-time morality. But while the spirit of Augustus' legislation, whether on marriage, child-bearing, crime, class distinction, or slavery, is essentially conservative, in accordance with the needs and wishes of his middle-class Italian supporters, Horace's appeal is more radical, and more romantic (lines 33-44):

> non his iuventus orta parentibus
> infecit aequor sanguine Punico,
>   Pyrrhumque et ingentem cecidit
>   Antiochum Hannibalemque dirum,
>
> sed rusticorum mascula militum
> proles, Sabellis docta ligonibus
>   versare glebas et severae
>   matris ad arbitrium recisos
>
> portare fustis, sol ubi montium
> mutaret umbras et iuga demeret
>   bobus fatigatis, amicum
>   tempus agens abeunte curru.

> (Not from such parents sprang the youth
> who stained the sea with Punic blood,
> who slaughtered the rulers of Syria,
> Macedon, and Carthage: but, men, born of
> yeoman soldiers, they learned to break
> up stubborn soil with Sabine mattocks;
> they cut the logs their stern mothers
> wanted, and shouldered them, as the sun
> made mountain shadows lengthen, releasing
> yokes from tired oxen. A kindly time was
> his departure.)

Horace was not much given to breaking stubborn clods or carrying firewood. He was "entirely aware of the difference between the strenuous life of those admirable *maiores* and his own delight in the leisure and peace afforded by an adequate country estate."[13] Yet a poet too honest to pretend that he would exchange his comfortable existence for the dour peasant's life, any more than Samuel Johnson considered remaining on Skye or Mull, may still sincerely and reasonably have believed that the peasant's bone-weariness had significant compensations that we with our "high standard of living" lack today. The Virgilian image of shadows

slowly falling from the mountains reminds us of the spiritual continuity perceived by Virgil between the three worlds, of the
Eclogues, half Italian, half in faerie; the *Georgics,* where simplicity and toil unite us with seasons, animals, and gods, and are revealed as the real foundation of Rome's greatness; and the *Aeneid,*
where Arcadian and Sabine virtues are symbolically combined,
and even Vulcan, as he begins work on Aeneas' shield (the glorious
future of Rome), is compared to an old farm woman rising before
dawn to begin her chores. There are no false notes here. If Virgil's message is romantic, it is also realistic: that unless we place
ourselves in harmony with nature—with the suffering she com-
mands, as well as the unexpected happiness she confers—we
cannot, personally, artistically, or as a society, create anything
worthwhile.

Now if the idealistic poet who aspires, as Blake did, to "build
Jerusalem / in England's green and pleasant land," turns his
gaze steadily to the "dark, Satanic mills," the private weaknesses
and the historical pressures by which we all are surrounded, there
is always the danger that his imagination will succumb to horror
and despair. This must have happened more than once to Virgil
and Horace. It is significant that the Roman Odes end, as the
Aeneid will, on a note of failure (III, 6, 45-48):

> damnosa quid non imminuit dies?
> aetas parentum peior avis tulit
>   nos nequiores, mox daturos
>   progeniem vitiosiorem.

> (Things decline as the days pass. Our
> fathers' time, inferior to theirs,
> produced descendants still worse, and
> we shall do the same.)

Golden dreams can fade, and bleak pessimism take over: what
Horace called *taedium.* Reformation was absolutely necessary;
absolute reformation was more than Augustus and the Roman
people were able, or willing, to accomplish. No matter how many
temples were rebuilt, marriage laws passed, titles declined, and
veterans hidden away in towns, old-time simplicity and virtue were
still as unrecoverable as the Golden Age itself; which myth accord-

ingly retains the meaning it was given, not in Eclogue 4, but in Epode 16: a *cri de coeur* at the unbridgeable gap between what ought to be and what unalterably is.

"The fundamental task of the imagination in ordinary life," says Northrup Frye, "is to produce, out of the society we have to live in, a vision of the society we want to live in. Obviously, that can't be a separated society, so we have to understand how to relate the two."[14]

How much Horace was torn between the will to "relate the two" and the feeling that this was impossible is reflected in the artful arrangement of Odes III, 1-6, by which parallels and contrasts are joined together in a complex but ordered structure, a lyric meditation on the meaning of Rome. So too, but on an infinitely larger scale, the analysis-defying architecture of Virgil's *Aeneid* balances epic and tragic vision, unity and disorder, meaning and meaninglessness, control and passion, accomplishment and desolation, within an overarching and final artistic order. The same ambiguity of feeling and purpose appears in simpler form in Livy's history. His principal aim, he states in his preface, is educational (*Praefatio*, 9-10):

Let each man, as he reads, direct his interest and thought to these questions: how men lived, how they behaved, and by what men and through what arts the power of our government was founded and increased both at home and in the field. Let him then follow, in his mind's eye, how that mode of life first, as it were, slips as self-control weakens, then totters more and more, and sets about its final headlong plunge, until the present era is reached, in which we can bear neither our faults nor their necessary cures. But what is especially wholesome and valuable to the understanding of affairs is that you may here perceive, clearly preserved to sight and memory, exemplary lessons of every kind, so that from this study you may distinguish those things which you and your country should imitate from those which, being ugly alike in their undertaking and their outcome, you should attempt by every means to avoid.

Livy wishes, ideally, by turning men's eyes to old Roman virtue, to support a renascence of old Roman greatness. At the same time, his Sallustian pessimism leads him to say, *in the same preface*, that his history will serve two altogether different purposes: to commemorate a mighty past, and to divert the writer's thought from the disastrous present.

Although, to return to the Roman Odes, most critics concede them flashes of inspiration—the description of Apollo in III, 4, or Regulus' leave-taking in III, 5, or the Sabine evening in III, 6— few have realized how much these odes are poetically charged as a group by Horace's uncertainty of mind. As Yeats said: "We make out of the quarrel with others, rhetoric, but out of the quarrel with ourselves, poetry." If Horace was able, though not so long or steadily as Virgil, yet in certain clear and exalted moments to perceive a harmony and order in the world by which private aspirations might be united with public ones, and even Roman history redeemed, he must also have frequently despaired of Rome's salvation and sensed the impossibility of reconciling personal happiness in any final way with the contemplation of and participation in historical reality. Precisely this alternation of feelings between hope and sadness, belief and unbelief, commitment and withdrawal, is the stuff of which genuine poetry is made, as much as death is, or love, or nature.

CHAPTER 5

Death, Time, and Love[1]

I Boundaries of Grief

THE honesty and courage with which Horace rejects inadequate or outgrown limits are most evident in his poems on death and change, especially against their Epicurean background. Lucretius had argued, in a peroration to his third book, on the soul, that "Death is nothing to us," since "we" lack sensation once body and soul atoms are disunited in death.[2] We may (said Lucretius) project our guilty consciences into imaginary tortures in Hell; we may "contaminate" the corpse with an impossible power of self-observation and suffering, imagining ourselves "to lie in cold obstruction and to rot"; or we may regret that someone's death has robbed him of life's pleasures, or that we ourselves shall some day be robbed of them: yet all these fears and griefs are irrational and silly, and should evaporate, like a child's fear of the dark, in the clear sunlight of Epicurean reason.

Yet the child's fear is not baseless, nor the grown man's. Lucretius recognized, correctly enough, that the fear of death as generally experienced arises largely from repression of guilt feelings or from unconscious self-deception. But even after neurotic anxiety, into which Lucretius had the insight of a great psychiatrist, is unmasked, and occasionally even cured, there still remains the universal or "existential" anxiety that Paul Tillich has described in *The Courage to Be*, which, whether of death or condemnation or meaninglessness, inheres inescapably in the human condition.[3] Where the psychoanalyst leaves off, the minister, says Tillich (and we might add, the lover and the poet) must begin. Otherwise, psychoanalysis, like many people's religion, may serve as a new and elaborate defense mechanism by which the realities of joy and suffering, love and death, are kept at bay.

Epicureanism claimed, as most philosophies do, to help men live in the present, by dispelling false desires and fears that disturb tranquility. Yet the clearest Epicurean message is a summons to escape from the dangerous immediacy of personal impulse into the eternal, stable world of impersonal process—the harbor or garden of the imagination. Lucretius never comes to grips with death as we know it: with what the death of a close relative or friend means to the survivor (however enlightened his mind), or with the impact on ourselves of the realization, which is *not* neurotic, that we carry our death within us. Love, too, he regards negatively, as an epiphenomenon of sexual lust, arising mainly from unreal imaginings and draining our resources, reputations, and bodies. As an antidote he recommends a kind of emotional sterilization, a participation of attitude in the safe atomic process of procreation, which may be attained by casually employing prostitutes to slake what Epicurus called a "natural and unnecessary" desire, or perhaps by drifting, if we are fortunate, into that habit of marital compatibility and affection which nature occasionally grants.[4]

Whether death, then, or love is in question, Epicurean tranquility presupposes our power and willingness to cut ourselves off from immediate and concrete experience.[5] The idea is common enough in philosophy, but in a doctrine based on pleasure it seems curiously misplaced: hence Cicero's very amusing comments in *De Finibus* on the discrepancy between the two meanings Epicureans gave to *voluptas*, pleasure as ordinarily experienced and lofty philosophical tranquility. The saint or poet—an Epicurus or a Lucretius—might reconcile the two. The ordinary Lucullus or Piso or Atticus never bothered.

Although Horace owed much to Epicureanism, he decidedly rejected any kind of tranquility that was reached by taking a detour around ordinary emotional experience, such as the fear of death. If in several satires and a few early odes, like II, 18, he raises the death's head to reveal the infatuation of avaricious, ambitious, and extravagant men, and to talk us into limiting our desires and our fears, death in his mature odes is no philosopher's cipher but a human reality with which we must personally and immediately come to terms. Once Horace himself was nearly killed by a falling tree. The incident, as described in Odes II, 13, impressed the *unpredict-*

ability of death on his mind: the way it is always at hand, cannot be eluded by normal, prudential measures, like avoiding war and the sea, and threatens the "pious" poet as well as the fool and criminal—however delightful the literary immortality he may anticipate. Accordingly, in some of the ripest, most beautiful odes of Books I-III, Horace takes up the assignment unfulfilled by Lucretius, of confronting a dear friend's death and the emotional certainty that he himself will die. If in these and other poems he achieves a balance of mind, however precarious, and a grasp of limit, however impermanent, not through bypassing human feeling and experience, but by opening himself to it, we must again admire and praise not just his sharp-eyed ironic intellect, but the deep courage with which the ironies he perceives in life are contemplated steadily and endured.

Thus in Odes I, 24, another fragment of his long conversation with Virgil, Horace refuses to employ the usual unthinking rhetoric of the *consolatio* form.

> Quis desiderio sit pudor aut modus
> tam cari capitis? praecipe lugubris
> cantus, Melpomene, cui liquidam pater
>   vocem cum cithara dedit.
>
> ergo Quintilium perpetuus sopor
> urget! cui Pudor et Iustitiae soror,
> incorrupta Fides, nudaque Veritas
>   quando ullum inveniet parem?
>
> multis ille bonis flebilis occidit,
> nulli flebilior quam tibi, Vergili.
> tu frustra pius heu non ita creditum
>   poscis Quintilium deos.
>
> quid si Threicio blandius Orpheo
> auditam moderere arboribus fidem,
> num vanae redeat sanguis imagini,
>   quam virga semel horrida,
>
> non lenis precibus fata recludere,
> nigro compulerit Mercurius gregi?
> durum: sed levius fit patientia
>   quidquid corrigere est nefas.

(How measure, how restrain our grief for
such a friend? Find out some strain of
melancholy song, sweet Muse, you who sing with
clear voice to the lyre.

So. Everlasting sleep weighs down Quintilius.
When shall Restraint, pure Faith, or naked
Honesty ever behold his equal?

Many good men wept at his death, none wept more
than you did, Virgil. Your loyalty's no good;
the gods won't give back what you owed them.

Say you could win all Nature's ear with sweeter
tunes than Orpheus played: would blood return to
that pale shade, once with his awful wand,
unmoved by prayers, Mercury shuts a new soul
into his black flock? Hard: but endurance makes
lighter what we may not correct.)

Although Quintilius is not mentioned until stanza 2, the opening
verses are essential. Consolations often begin with the commonplace, that grief is permissible; but usually, as in the dignified letter of Servius Sulpicius to Cicero on his daughter's death,[6] this
concession is followed by a series of arguments showing why
mourning should be restrained and finite. Lucretius too follows
convention when he criticizes, though not without sympathy, the
man who accepts no limit of mourning (III, 907-8):

> insatiabiliter deflevimus, aeternumque
> nulla dies nobis maerorem e pectore demet.

> (Our indefatigable tears of sorrow Time
> everlasting will not take away.)

Horace transfers *desiderium* from its principal Lucretian meaning,[7] of the desire for good things that dead men never feel (a
point intended to comfort us), to the passion with which we, the
living, miss the dead. How should this passion be limited, and with
what right? In Odes I, 24, he seeks a twofold *modus*: first, the
expression of grief in poetry—for the collocation of sounds, *sit
pudor, aut modus, tam cari capitis,* suggests the "lump in the
throat," the uncommunicative stammering of a grief too deep for

words; but also (since words imply meaning) some definition of brute experience, some understanding that might be reached through poetry.

Definition will not be premature. Harsh ironies must first be stated, emotional rebellion given rein. The comparison of death to sleep is familiar and could be comforting if *urget*, emphasized by enjambement, did not change it suddenly to a nightmare in which the sleeper is "pressed down," trying to awake but unable. Like Virgil's *somnus ferreus* ("iron sleep"),[8] the metaphor revives our instinctive horror at the idea of sinking into nothingness, like "patients etherized upon a table." Again, recollection of the dead man's virtues is a consolatory commonplace: but as they pass before our minds, like beautiful, serene ladies, we realize all the more poignantly how unique and irreplaceable Horace and Virgil felt Quintilius to be. The dignified restraint so needed by the survivors seemed, ironically, to have died with him. Something of his *veritas*, however, reappears in Horace's insistence on just those aspects of death that deny us consolation. That is "naked honesty."[9]

Turning to Virgil, around whom his thoughts and the poem center, Horace identifies him once more with his hero, Aeneas. *Tu frustra pius.* Virgil's faithful devotion meets with no reward, no response in heaven. The words,

> non ita creditum
> poscis Quintilium deos,

with their echo of Odes I, 3, 5-6, where Virgil was entrusted to the ship,

> navis, quae tibi creditum
> debes Vergilium,

mark the continuity both of Horace's love for Virgil and his foreboding that Virgil's heroism of mind will come to nothing. The phrase, *non ita creditum,* is highly ironic. By its more obvious, conventional meaning, life is a loan, not a gift—and death therefore a necessary end that "will come when it will come." A second meaning is less reassuring. The gods, unlike Virgil's ship, will not meet the obligation that human trust imposes. Prayer and sacrifice, like devotion, are unavailing.

Two further allusions press home the point. The first is to Virgil's poetry. In Georgics 4, Eurydice could not, finally, be restored to Orpheus, though his devout lyre roused the nether gods to compassion. The second recalls Horace's own early verses on Mercury (Odes I, 10, 17-20):

> tu pias laetis animas reponis
> sedibus virgaque levem coerces
> aurea turbam, superis deorum
> gratus et imis.

> (Devoted souls you lead to seats of joy, your
> golden wand restrains the insignificant
> multitude, all of the gods are pleased.)

The stanza, like the entire hymn, is gay and fanciful. Like a lictor who knows his business, Mercury ushers the better class of souls to their reserved seats in Elysium, keeping the general mob in place. But although the frequency in Horace's odes of this "Elysian" motif, often conveyed in images of gold and music, shows the strength and consistency of his feeling that the poet is distinguished from other men, even after death, by his peculiar *pietas*, we must not infer from this that Horace had any definite religious belief in an afterlife. Nobody, however *pius,* can be exempted personally from the power of death. That is why Mercury's wand is, in the present ode, not golden but awful.

What *modus* then remains, after so many consolations are rejected? There is, first, nature's own relief. Suffering grows lighter (*levius,* contrast *urget*) after we have mourned long and fully for the dead person and for the disruption in death of our accustomed hopes and aspirations. Second, by refusing, with Horace, to accept the abstract and impersonal limit of mourning dictated by philosophy or social convention, we rediscover the true meaning and force of the old heroic virtue of endurance (*tlêmosynê, patientia*). But third: by completing his ode Horace not only expresses his grief but reaches a true natural limit or *modus* in which heart and mind may acquiesce. In other odes, he urges his friends, like Plancus, not to pass the natural boundaries of grief: for skies are not always cloudy, rain falls not forever, and man too must yield to time and change. Yet Horace himself never yields without a struggle. Death *is* something to him: not a problem to be solved, but a reality to be lived with. Man's fate cannot be "corrected" as critics like Quintilius correct inadequate poetic efforts. Yet this incorrigibility imposes its own *modus*, which must suffice.

II *Secondary Limits of Enjoyment*

To Epicurus, the certainty of dying was a reminder to live. "We are born once, twice we cannot be, but for endless time are doomed not to exist: yet you, who control not the morrow, keep putting off happiness."[10] This statement was not meant to contradict the other, that "death is nothing to us"; for if, as Nature remarks in Lucretius' poem, a man has enjoyed life's bounty, gratitude and simple decency bid him depart when the time comes like a satisfied guest—while if he is not satisfied, he "never could be, though he lived forever!"[11] But what if Epicurus were wrong, and length of time made a difference to pleasure? Is the prospect of death really "nothing to us"? Horace was deeply impressed by Lucretius' renewal of the old banquet analogy, and he made it his own, along with the more obvious rule of *decorum* that youth should have its fling and old age keep a discreet distance from revels; and yet, something in him agreed with the fool satirized by Lucretius who grows maudlin in his cups and cries, "Let us drink, for life is short!"[12] The raising of the death's head may as easily lead men to folly as to wisdom, and spoil, even as it intensifies, their search for present happiness.

Where, then, in relation to Epicurus, but also to the vulgar City Mouse, does Horace place himself at table? His famous recommendation to "pluck the day," *carpe diem,* is really two-edged. On the one hand, the gardening metaphor suggests, as in Shakespeare's Histories, a natural sanity and order that men should imitate.[13] But if we replant the phrase in its context, in Odes I, 11, the effect is different. Horace is advising a girl, Leuconoe (whose name may imply simple-mindedness) not to bother with astrology or worry about the hour of her death, but take life as it comes:

> Tu ne quaesieris, scire nefas, quem mihi, quem tibi
> finem di dederint, Leuconoe, nec Babylonios
> temptaris numeros. ut melius, quidquid erit, pati,
> seu pluris hiemes seu tribuit Iuppiter ultimam,

quae nunc oppositis debilitat pumicibus mare
Tyrrhenum: sapias, vina liques, et spatio brevi
spem longam reseces. dum loquimur, fugerit invida
aetas: carpe diem, quam minimum credula postero.

> (Never inquire, Leuconoee,
> what end is fixed for you or me.
> Better to take life's any line
> regardless of astrology,
> whether the fates more years assign
> or this winter must be the last
> to tire out the Etruscan brine
> by flinging it against the cliffs:
> be sensible, and strain your wine;
> time's short, so prune those farflung ifs.
> We talk, the present turns to past:
> pluck the day, then, and hold it fast!)[14]

The dramatic situation is amusing. Leuconoe's adviser has a vested interest in her cooperating with nature, gathering rosebuds while she may. They will go to bed together—not exactly a moral for schoolboys.[15] There is even a hint that Leuconoe will not trust the next *lover* (not *day*) so easily. More seriously, though, the natural backdrop for lovemaking is time's brutality, which wears us out, as the sea beats against the cliff.[16] Surely one obvious response is to hold life tighter, with the urgency of Catullus making love (in Poem 5),

> Vivamus, mea Lesbia, atque amemus
>
> (Let's live, dear Lesbia, and love. . . .)

Although Horace seldom makes war on time, as Catullus does, or Donne, and is too polite to "rage against the dying of the light," he must constantly contend with the urgent wish, not to pluck the flower of life, but to rend or snatch it hastily. Once more: whatever definitions of attitude and behavior the Odes reveal are secondary limits, or *modi*, neither reached without rebellion of heart nor meaningful apart from the metaphorical, tonal, and dramatic context through which they are conveyed.

Consider, for example, how the initial admonition in Odes II, 3, to keep a "balanced mind" in good times and bad, is given a new

complexity of meaning by Horace's passionate awareness of how
swiftly time flies:

> Aequam memento rebus in arduis
> servare mentem, non secus in bonis
>   ab insolenti temperatam
>   laetitia, moriture Delli,
>
> seu maestus omni tempore vixeris,
> seu te in remoto gramine per dies
>   festos reclinatum bearis
>   interiore nota Falerni.
>
> quo pinus ingens albaque populus
> umbram hospitalem consociare amant
>   ramis? quid obliquo laborat
>   lympha fugax trepidare rivo?
>
> huc vina et unguenta et nimium brevis
> flores amoenae ferre iube rosae,
>   dum res et aetas et sororum
>   fila trium patiuntur atra.
>
> cedes coemptis saltibus et domo
> villaque flavus quam Tiberis lavit;
>   cedes, et exstructis in altum
>   divitiis potietur heres.
>
> divesne prisco natus ab Inacho
> nil interest an pauper et infima
>   de gente sub divo moreris,
>   victima nil miserantis Orci.
>
> omnes eodem cogimur, omnium
> versatur urna serius ocius
>   sors exitura et nos in aeternum
>   exilium impositura cumbae.

(In uphill efforts still maintain a balanced mind; in good times, too, moderate
exultation, for, Dellius, you are bound to
die, whether you live in constant sadness,
or lie down in a quiet glade, drinking
holiday cheer from precious, specially
saved champagne.

Why do the white poplar and tall pine inter-
lace their friendly shade affectionately?
Or brooks frantically rush from bank to bank?
Call for some wine, for perfumes; call for
lovely roses, so short-lived, while your
condition, age, and the black Sisters give
you leave.

From purchased fields you will depart. Your
house, your Tiber-washed estate will see you
go, and your heir will drink up all that deep-
piled wealth. Whether of Argive lineage you're
born, or, a low beggar, you die in the open
air, death doesn't mind class distinctions.
We all go the same way, we all are named on
lots that someday fall out of the urn, call-
ing us to sail away to endless exile.)

On first reading, death's inevitability points a simple moral. Who,
with happiness within his grasp, will live in perpetual melancholy?
The quiet countryside, the holiday, the wine recall Lucretius'
idyllic picture of the men who enjoy lying on soft grass by a river
bank or under the branches of a tall tree when the season smiles
and it is spring.[17] Lucretius, of course, was showing how effortlessly true pleasure is secured. But Horace not only replaces water
with wine, and Falernian at that, and of a choice vintage (*interi-
ore nota*); he turns an ironic, dubious glance upon the pleasure
seeker as well as his foil, the melancholy man. Does it matter in
the end which choice is made?

The following appeal to nature's example is ambivalent too.
Trees are reliable enough guides; and the pine and poplar em-
bracing each other with their branches (note the sound pattern-
ing, the favorite image of "interlacing") evidently furnish an
object lesson in leisurely companionship. Yet the rushing brook,
while it illustrates the comic pointlessness of our hustling and
bustling, may teach, as well, that effort, trepidation, and flight are
as natural as quiet sociability. In the faster tempo of stanza 4, the
peremptory summons to enjoy life now, amid wine, perfume, and
roses—for men, like flowers, are short-lived, and old time is still
a-flying—do we not hear the rushing of the brook?

The reality of death complicates, as it dwarfs, any lesson of right living. In stanzas 5-7 Horace pulls out all the emotional stops, the imagery of urn, boat, and exile, and repetition of sound, not so much to impress Dellius, though the kick may have done him good, as to express his own knowledge that death will come whether you are sad or happy, rich or poor, Dellius or Horace, and to permit the feelings that naturally accompany such a realization to find, through a slightly humorous self-exaggeration, their proper *modus*. The dramatic contrast between the "trepidation" of verses 11-16 and the slowing down and steadying of rhythm in 17-28 suggest a corresponding inward motion, towards steadiness of mind; for under death's shadow the *aequa mens* requested earlier is revealed as a momentary triumph of balance, a juggling act with human passions kept successfully in play.

As Horace's other metaphor, *mentem temperatam*, once more suggests, every "solution" or resolution in the Odes is unique. Thus Odes II, 11, which also concerns death, seems on first reading to repeat the lesson of II, 3; but on closer observation, its metaphorical and dramatic tendency is very different.

> Quid bellicosus Cantaber et Scythes,
> Hirpine Quincti, cogitet Hadria
>   divisus obiecto, remittas
>   quaerere, nec trepides in usum
>
> poscentis aevi pauca: fugit retro
> levis iuventas et decor, arida
>   pellente lascivos amores
>   canitie facilemque somnum.
>
> non semper idem floribus est honor
> vernis, neque uno Luna rubens nitet
>   vultu: quid aeternis minorem
>   consiliis animum fatigas?
>
> cur non sub alta vel platano vel hac
> pinu iacentes sic temere et rosa
>   canos odorati capillos,
>   dum licet, Assyriaque nardo
>
> potamus uncti? dissipat Euhius
> curas edaces. quis puer ocius
>   restinguet ardentis Falerni
>   pocula praetereunte lympha?

quis devium scortum eliciet domo
Lyden? eburna dic age cum lyra
   maturet in comptum Lacaenae
    more comas religata nodum.

(Don't worry, Quinctius, about Spanish or
Scythian plans of war. Set apart by the
sea, you needn't fret or fear to enjoy
a life that asks but little. Youth lightly flees, and propriety, once our gray
hairs repel the play of love and the ease
of sleep. Spring flowers do not always
bloom perfectly, or the red-hued moon
shine without changing: why then weary
yourself with endless thoughts?

Why not lie, so, under the plane tree or
the pine (be bold!), and perfuming gray
hair with roses, anointing us with costly
nard, drink while we may? Dionysus scatters
pursuing cares. What boy will intercept
some water more quickly now, to put out this
wine? Who will draw out the recherché play-
girl, Lyde? Tell her to come quick with her
ivory lyre, hair bound up in the Spartan
mode.)

Through the third stanza and into the fourth, Horace's intention
seems as steady as his tone. As nature's boundaries set Italy apart
from Spain or Scythia, so Quinctius should detach himself from
far-off worries and follow nature's injunction to enjoy life a little.
As ever, the lesson is sound. Like Dellius and other hyperactive,
neurotic people, Quinctius would profit from the attitude of relaxation that Horace so tactfully yet firmly leads him to adopt.
In stanza 4, however, the latent opposition between the precept
of leisurely relaxation and the feelings normally induced by nature's swift changes comes to the fore in rich, sensual images and
a speeding up of rhythm. Decorum is now "put to flight" in a new
sense as the gray-haired men wreath their heads rebelliously with
garlands of sweet-smelling, luxurious roses. And other symbolic
acts of defiance follow. The elaborate epithets and descriptive
phrases more than give concreteness to an abstract theme: rather,

the rich Assyrian nard, the blazing Falernian wine, the gifted play-mate with her ivory lyre introduce into the ode a new atmosphere of beauty, luxury, and sensuality, in which precepts of moderation and restraint must be lost to view. The pastoral scene has become a carousal.

The urgency Horace feels in nature is reflected in the staccato brevity of *dum licet* (the City Mouse's phrase), *ocius, maturet.* A battle is turning. Worries, evidently of death, are routed: not by the radiant sun shafts of Epicurean reason, but by the compulsion of inner warmth and intoxication. We may compare Verdi's grand scene in which Falstaff, drinking wine, gradually puts off the chill of Thames water, defeat, and mortality. Precisely the same feeling is depicted in Horace's "Soracte Ode," I, 9, where the chill of body and spirit induced by winter and by wintry thoughts of old age and death is overcome by fire and wine and the grateful acceptance of the present moment. Yet the movement of feeling dramatized in Odes I, 9, as in II, 11, contradicts its philosophical lesson. Is it acceptance of the present (and resignation to the future) or *flight into the present* that brings a symbolic summertime of the spirit? The two seem inseparably joined.

In the present ode, decorum and sense return where we would least expect them, in mid-revel. Although the question, *quis puer ocius*, hints at renewed competition with youth, Horace will symbolically water down his fiery wine to a moderate blend. Similarly, an ultimate order and restraint may be seen in the description of Lyde. Her ivory lyre, however luxurious, is still an instrument that produces harmony. Her hair style will have sex appeal (indeed, Horace's senses seem often to have been aroused by the way a woman's hair falls along the back of the neck); yet the secret of her attractiveness is an artful neatness. She is *simplex munditiis*: so was Pyrrha; and so, once again, are Horace's poetry and his life. Earlier, his feeling of time's urgency led him to violate the spirit of his own injunction,

> nec trepides in usum
> poscentis aevi pauca.

Now, as Lyde's hair is bound back into a simple but elegant knot (*nodus*), Horace's pursuit of happiness is likewise gathered into a harmonious and reflective attitude in which urgency and haste are no longer perceptible. Only in this way does he reach a secondary limit of attitude, a final but decorous relaxation.

While Horace searches constantly for what I have called secondary limit, each of his poems is unique in its shaping mood, the pattern it forms, and the resolution, if any, at which it arrives. The arrangement of the Odes emphasizes difference: for example, juxtaposing Odes II ,13, which ends with a cheerful fantasy of the afterlife, and the grim and ironic Ode II, 14, where an heir is ultimately judged "worthier" because he pours out his father's long-hoarded treasures of wine. Differences of mood and attitude also act over larger distances, defying generalization. We might easily regard Odes III, 29, to Maecenas, as a philosophical epilogue to the Odes because of its position and because Horace speaks as one who has achieved self-sufficiency and independence of fortune even in the realm (symbolized by the sea) most exposed to natural and historical catastrophe. Part Epicurean, but also part Stoic in color, the ode foreshadows Horace's attempt in the Epistles to give philosophical autonomy and stability to an emotionally disordered life. Yet, had the state of mind shown in Odes III, 29 remained constant, the introspective struggle of the Epistles would hardly have been necessary. That is why it is instructive to turn from Odes III, 29 to a poem like II, 6, where the oppressive pervading atmosphere of weariness and decay is relieved only by the humor of exaggeration. Septimius, young and energetic, has made the conventional friendly offer to follow Horace anywhere, but the poet designates Tibur as the "resting place" of his old age, "a home for one weary of the sea, of roads, of warfare." Or, if sickness grows worse, he will go south . . . and his thoughts linger comfortably on blanketed sheep, good honey, olives, wine, a warm winter, and a prolonged spring. There he will die—but with, as it were, his *rosa sera*. The ode ends with a sentimental fancy. Septimius will prove his friendship after all—by weeping over the ashes of his "poet friend." Although he parodies Catullus here, Horace seems unable to throw off Catullan melancholy. But far from canceling out Odes III, 29, II, 6 actually gives it point: for self-sufficiency and evenness of temper mean more to us, and seem more capable of imitation, if their famed exponent sometimes felt sorry for himself or rebelled at heart against the laws of nature that simple politeness bids us accept without complaint.

III   *Love and Time*

The passion evoked by natural change also colors Horace's odes on love, making them more than playful exercises in disengaged irony. They do, of course, display variations of well-known and trite Hellenistic patterns: the "chain of love," where nobody's affection is reciprocated; the "hard" youth or maiden, who will eventually fall in love and repent of earlier unkindness; the unwary novice, who has much to learn; the "farewell to love" that never quite comes off, and so forth. But while Horace continues to be amused at love's changes, the statement in Odes I, 6 quoted earlier, that "even aflame, my heart is easy and peaceful,"

> sive quid urimur
> non praeter solitum leves,

applies better to the playful epodes, 11, 14, and 15, than to the riper odes.

Consider first Odes I, 33 to Tibullus, the elegiac poet. As, in the Strauss opera *Ariadne auf Naxos*, Zerbinetta's troupe dances a wild comic pantomime of love's inconstancy to divert Ariadne from her stonelike grief at having been betrayed by Theseus, Horace attempts to cheer up Tibullus by reminding him of what he already knows, and knows Horace knows he knows: the ridiculousness of love.

> Albi, ne doleas plus nimio memor
> immitis Glycerae neu miserabilis
> decantes elegos, cur tibi iunior
>   laesa praeniteat fide,
>
> insignem tenui fronte Lycorida
> Cyri torret amor, Cyrus in asperam
> declinat Pholoen; sed prius Apulis
>   iungentur capreae lupis,
>
> quam turpi Pholoe peccet adultero.
> sic visum Veneri, cui placet imparis
> formas atque animos sub iuga aenea
>   saevo mittere cum ioco.

ipsum me melior cum peteret Venus,
grata detinuit compede Myrtale
libertina, fretis acrior Hadriae
curvantis Calabros sinus.

(Just so you won't miss your sweetheart
more than too much, Tibullus, or complain of broken faith when she chooses a
younger man: Lycoris of the slender brow
burns for Cyrus, who swerves after hard
Pholoê: but sooner will she-goats be wed
to wolves than Pholoê entertain disgrace.
So Venus wills, whom it delights to force
unequal shapes and minds under the same
cruel yoke. I myself had a nicer call, but
stuck it out with Myrtalê, a girl sharp as
the Adriatic pitching its splendid curves.)

Tibullus was well aware, from reading and experience, of the
dance patterns lovers make, their disparities of condition and
affection, and the uncontrollable "swerve" of mind or fortune by
which their lot is (momentarily) determined. His elegies are
ironic from start to finish because of the contrast they exploit between the calm, artistic intellect and the troubled heart; for he
wanted Delia, of the blond hair and slender arms, to reciprocate
his devotion, but knew she never could, and he wanted a lasting
union of sentiment and passion in a real, Roman world that must
destroy—as it did for Catullus—every idealistic dream.[18] His Hellenistic consciousness of the dance patterns of love therefore en-
forces, not impairs, the sincerity and seriousness of his feeling.

That is why Horace recommends no simple boundary for lov-
ing—a thing which, as Terence's Parmeno remarks, is necessarily
excessive, defying rhyme and reason[19]—but just not to grieve
"more than too much." If the final comparison of Myrtalê to the
dangerous, unpredictable sea shows an ironic awareness of love's
deceptiveness (much as, in Odes I, 5, the older, wiser poet observes
a naive young man on the verge of emotional shipwreck with
Pyrrha), the sensual image, not just of stormy waters but a woman's swelling bosom,

fretis acrior Hadriae
curvantis Calabros sinus,

[100]

shows how susceptible Horace's own senses are, and more important, his imagination. He too can be swept away by beauty beyond the bounds of reason. He writes, therefore, not to disagree with Tibullus' perception of love, but to remind him, with fondness and compassion, that mourning is a one-sided reaction. "See how I can accept nature's game, in fairly good humor. You have my sympathy, have some of my happiness too."

Complaining was not Horace's style. Yet his heart often rebelled against the cruelty, not of a mistress—for he never gave full devotion, like Catullus and the elegists, to a single woman—but of the laws of change by which human life is governed. In love's realm, as elsewhere, he reaches out despite his better judgment for the unattainable, the *rosa sera*.

Thus, in Odes I, 13, we see one Horace at the wrong end of a love triangle, jealously resenting Lydia's attentions to young, athletic Telephus, while a second Horace looks on with keen-eyed detachment; but in stanzas 4 and 5, a third, more complex attitude emerges:

> non, si me satis audias,
> speres perpetuum dulcia barbare
>   laedentem oscula quae Venus
> quinta parte sui nectaris imbuit.
>   felices ter et amplius
> quos irrupta tenet copula nec malis
>   divulsus querimoniis
> suprema citius solvet amor die.

> (If you'd listen to me—he'll not forever inflict pain on those tenderest lips
> Venus' nectar has ever touched. Blessed
> are they whose bond continues tight. No
> ill complaints set them asunder; they'll
> be joined in love till the last day.

Although Horace asserts, with the ironic certainty of an *erôtodidaskalos*, or professor of erotic science, that love is, like youth, "a thing will not endure," his feelings can evidently still be engaged; for his "if you'd listen to me—" betrays a hope that, experience to the contrary, his confession of Lydia's tender charms and his contrasting of Telephus' impetuous violence with his own gentler affection will turn not just Lydia's ears but her whole feeling toward himself. Once recognized as foolish, this hope calls up an ironic yet heartfelt statement of what lovers ideally want: to be joined to their mistresses in an unbroken bond to the end of time. The wish, as it is phrased, indicates its own impossibility of fulfillment. As the sexual *copula* cannot be prolonged indefinitely, but in its climax brings dissolution and renewed separation and loneliness, so the most intense emotional bond cannot be counted on to last forever. And yet: the present indicative, *tenet*, argues that "marriages of true minds" do occur, if only in rare and beautiful instances. Are the elegists, then, right in their romantic quest for constancy of passion? Or (since *querimoniae* is used of elegiac laments as well as lovers' quarrels) is Horace implying that love endures only when the heart's passion is transmuted into the more stable condition of charitable affection? Can the lover's romantic dream of permanence be realized only when sexual passion is sublimated, and eros denied?

One alternative, certainly, to the elegiac view of love is the pastoral. This is best represented in Odes I, 17, where Horace invites Tyndaris to share his refuge from destructive passion—from the "wolf," Cyrus, who would "tear her undeserving clothes." In the pastoral world, love is always a wolf among the sheep, a cold wind among the flowers. It can be admitted only in the tame, pastoralized form of general charitable benevolence. Like the Tin Woodman of Oz, the poet-shepherd must "have no heart." As Theocritus and Virgil, then, live midway between fashionable urban flirtation and tragic self-abandonment, being sensitive to matters of the heart and deeply compassionate, but never surrendering themselves altogether to passion (as Daphnis does in the myth, or Catullus and the elegists in real life), so Horace walks a tightrope between callousness and desolation. Again and again, his poems show how much the elegists' dream attracted him; again and again, he gives the lie to his own pose of emotional detachment; yet he generally returns from sympathetic involvement in the passion of love to the re-establishment in himself of that sensitive yet tranquil state of mind that owes so much to Virgil's pastoral teaching.

Whatever challenges tranquility, though, renews the poetic impulse. Once it is activated, Horace's emotional reaction to decay

and death gives color and excitement to an ode like II, 5, making
it a companion piece to poems like II, 3 and II, 11:

> Nondum subacta ferre iugum valet
> cervice, nondum munia comparis
>   aequare nec tauri ruentis
>   in venerem tolerare pondus.
>
> circa virentis est animus tuae
> campos iuvencae, nunc fluviis gravem
>   solantis aestum, nunc in udo
>   ludere cum vitulis salicto
>
> praegestientis. tolle cupidinem
> immitis uvae: iam tibi lividos
>   distinguet Autumnus racemos
>   purpureo varius colore.
>
> iam te sequetur: currit enim ferox
> aetas et illi quos tibi dempserit
>   apponet annos; iam proterva
>   fronte petet Lalage maritum,
>
> dilecta quantum non Pholoe fugax,
> non Chloris albo sic umero nitens
>   ut pura nocturno renidet
>   luna mari, Cnidiusve Gyges,
>
> quem si puellarum insereres choro,
> mire sagaces falleret hospites
>   discrimen obscurum solutis
>   crinibus ambiguoque vultu.

(She cannot yet support the yoke required,
nor handle her part beneath, bearing the
brunt of the bull's onerous, plunging lust.
Your heifer's thoughts ramble about the grassy
fields: in rivers now she likes to elude the
heat, or fool around with the young calves
in pleasant thickets. Don't desire the unripe grape. Wait, and shortly brilliant autumn
will dye your blue clusters a deep purple.
Shortly, her steps will follow yours [time runs
terribly], gaining all the years you lose; Lal-
agê *will* solicit a mate, shortly—

loved as Pholoê never was, or Chloris, whose
gleaming shoulder shone like the moon at
night over the sea, or young Gyges,
who, set in a dance, could fool keen ob-
servers [is it a girl or a boy?] with his
flowing hair and deceptive countenance.)

Horace begins, as often, by stating the rules of the game. He is an
experienced umpire, an *erôtodidaskalos* in the long line that begins with Anacreon and moves, through Callimachus, to its culmination in Ovid. And the lesson is the same as in other odes, whether to a young "filly" now ready for sex, an older woman whose time
has passed, or a proud beauty who will some day become that older
woman and be sorry she once treated her lovers (especially poets)
so shabbily. Ripeness is all, in vegetable and animal life, and in
human. The comparison of the present girl, first to a heifer, then
to an unripe grape, is humorous and dispassionate: we smile as we
see her sporting on the verge of adult sexuality.

This initial humor implies Horace's own acceptance of natural
change; but as he urges the banishing of unseasonable desire,
his reassurances become dubious and self-contradictory. At first
glance, *iam tibi ... iam te sequetur* conveys a tranquilizing promise. Time will work, the girl grow, for the man's benefit (dative of
the patient lover into whose hands all things will be delivered).
By the usual, ironic reversal, she who was pursued will pursue in
turn. Yet autumn, the "season of mists and mellow fruitfulness," is
also the time when days shorten, and winter and death draw near;
and the autumn of promise in which the girl will blossom into
womanhood is also the autumn of Horace's life—for Horace, we
now realize, is the teacher and the lover, too. His promise to himself is therefore illusory. Lalage will "follow" him only in time;
and time, as it runs, is correctly perceived not as *ferax,* or "fruitful," but as *ferox,* "wild and cruel." The conceit, that time will
add to the girl the years it "takes from" her lover, shows the fallacy
of wishful thinking, for the two will never meet, the one ripening,
the other growing younger, in an ideal balance. There will instead be a new and worse disparity. Venus can be very funny—and
very cruel. A third *iam,* a third future indicative, *petet,*[20] shows
that Horace will be betrayed by the movement of time that seemed

to favor him, for once ripe, Lalage will seek a husband, pursuing him with her beautiful face as an animal (the comedy continues) attacks with its forehead: but the man she will attract, or attack, will not be Horace.

So far, the situational irony is Hellenistic, resembling that of the "farewell to passion." Yet the very effort of Horace's protestations and struggle for self-control makes us feel how much he is surprised, and his normal defensive irony overwhelmed, by the violence of his feeling. Not the lighter odes on love, but poems like II, 3 and II, 11 on change and death offer the best parallel. Here, as there, the heart's rebellion must seek and find its own *modus*, a limit heretofore undefined by poetic convention or philosophical instruction.

What happens is surprising. With *dilecta*, Horace's imagination turns symbolically from the future to the past, reawakening earlier memories: of the elusive Pholoe; of Chloris, her shoulder gleaming like the moon at night (so Sappho recalls a beloved girl, now far away); or Gyges with his perfect girlish beauty. As Horace's thoughts recede, so does the passion that the comparisons seemed designed to enhance. The ending is a *discrimen obscurum*, a solution hard to discern correctly. At first, the images of the moon and Gyges' deceptive face seem to emphasize the unattainable aspect of love. The heightened, lyrical tone of

> ut pura nocturno renidet
> luna mari,

contrasts altogether with the humorous, common-sensical description of the heifer and the unripe grape, so that we might compare

> mitte sectari, rosa quo locorum
> sera moretur;

but Odes II, 5 does not end like I, 38 with the acceptance of present reality. Instead, the final action takes place in the imperfect subjunctive, in dream and idea. Yet the steadying of rhythm in the last two stanzas suggests that Horace finally achieves tranquility, as immediate passion fades into images of more distant beauty: not so much escaping from feeling, as moving, somewhat like Plato's philosophical lover, from the immediate sensual response to one person's physical charms to the broader and deeper contemplation of Beauty itself. It is this refining of passion through art and thought into a pure and lasting form that, finally, is symbolized by the moon, pure and beautiful through its changes, and by the equally virginal image of Gyges that the memory retains. Just so, in Odes III, 13, the sacrifice of a warm-blooded kid to the cool, refreshing *fons Bandusia* is a metaphor of the way in which art heals passion, and makes it whole, while giving it permanence.[21] Nonetheless, the ending of Odes II, 5 remains ambiguous, like Gyges' countenance; we do not know exactly what has become of Horace's passion; and we can understand why he is not just being ironic when, in the Epistles, he looks back on the Odes as *ludicra*, or "playthings," in which life's problems never received the critical diagnosis, or the permanent and reliable remedy, that only philosophy can offer.

CHAPTER 6

Philosophical Interlude[1]

I *Renunciation of Playthings*

STEADINESS of mind is more easily recommended to others than gained for ourselves. Those who have failed but kept trying will be encouraged by the perseverance of Horace, who retired to the Sabine farm in 23 or 22 B.C. to study philosophy, yet confesses a few years later that he is further from the goal than ever (in Epistles I, 8, to Celsus, cited in Chapter 1):

> Muse, take a message. Happiness and luck to
> Celsus A., Tiberius' friend and scribe. Say, if
> he asks, despite great resolutions I'm neither
> virtuous nor happy—not that hail has battered my
> vines, heat killed my olives, or some plague broken
> out among my cattle: but *I'm* unwell, in mind more
> than physique; can't stand to hear or learn what
> might relieve me; resent trusted doctors, get cross
> at friends for warding off death-bringing lethargy;
> pursue known harm, run from expected help; at Rome,
> want Tibur, and at Tibur, Rome.
>
> Then ask: is *he* in health? Successful? Happy?
> Does he get on with T.? With his companions? If
> he replies, "Just fine," be glad; but later see you
> instill this lesson in his ear: "CELSUS, IF YOU
> CAN BEAR GOOD LUCK, WE'LL BEAR WITH YOU."

It would be wrong to read Horace's description of his spiritual malaise as a tactful *me quoque*, a sweetening of his recommendation of modesty to Celsus (who probably needed it). The point is that Horace saw his personal struggle as having universal significance. Like all truisms, the "medicinal power of philosophy" has little meaning unless we realize that only philosophy can save us from succumbing by insensible stages to a spiritual lethargy or coma (*veternus*). Horace appreciated but was also human enough to resent the Socratic gadfly that awakens minds; and his philosophical epistles educate, as the Odes do, by a double movement from the personal to the general, and back again; like Johnson's essays, too, of which Professor Bate has written,

We can tell ourselves what is true and desirable while we are also telling others, particularly if we are emphasizing not one but two or more aspects of a matter. Indeed, we may question whether what we are telling others will have the desired persuasiveness unless we are also telling ourselves.[2]

Again, the Epistles, like Johnson's essays (and the Odes) "persuade because nothing that can attract the human imagination or bias judgment is ever lightly or easily dismissed."[3] Behind the recommendations of simplicity and equanimity there always lingers the *rosa sera*, or *atra Cura*. Though not immodest like Celsus, or neurasthenic like Tibullus, or a harassed businessman like Torquatus, Horace knew from his own experience the "treachery of the human heart" by which all men are sometimes betrayed, losing the good life that seemed within their grasp. Since the deepest, most personal wants of Celsus, Tibullus, and Torquatus are our own, as is the motor instability of Bullatius, in Epistles I, 11, or the complaint of the steward, in I, 14, or since (to take a problem that came to a head after 23 B.C.) the bitterness and resentment menacing Horace's exemplary relationship with Maecenas lurk behind every kind of social intercourse, Horace is most classical not by ignoring particulars but by seeing universals through them. Beginning usually by portraying some particular crisis or state of mind (his own, or another's) acutely but sympathetically, he reaches out toward enduring generalizations about human nature and conduct in the light of which he, his friends, and posterity may lead better lives and win a surer, more objective foundation of happiness.

In the dedicatory Epistle, I, 1, he compares himself to a retiring gladiator and tired race horse and then explains his purpose (lines 10-12):

> nunc itaque et versus et cetera ludicra pono;
> quid verum atque decens curo et rogo et omnis
> in hoc sum;
> condo et compono quae mox depromere possim.
>
> (Poems and other playthings I renounce. What's
> true and proper is my whole concern, storing
> provisions up against the future.)

The idea is still ironic. Poetry is no "child's play," and the Epistles are evidently poetry (consider their diction, the controlled and varied rhythm, and the guidance of thought through metaphor, as well as the many lyrical "purple passages"). Yet Horace is often most serious when he reports a change of mind. Perhaps, as he read and reread Plato's dialogues, he became convinced that the search for truth (*philosophia*) should precede artistic creation; that the resolutions offered by lyric poetry were "playful" and inadequate, because they were momentary; and that some more constant steadying of purpose was now required.[4] Advancing years demanded, if not the total abnegation of creativity, at least a symbolic change of rhythm.

Significantly, Horace felt a new attraction to Stoicism in these years. Terms like *virtus, vitium, peccare, recte,* and *stultus* recur frequently and seriously in the Epistles. Before, the Stoic preacher was ridiculed as a fool and madman; now his voice blends with that of the satirist in a reconciliation that anticipates Persius. Too, Horace's frequent citation of *res* as the enemy suggests a real fear of being overwhelmed by material possessions. To a man of forty-three, sick, uncertain, and burdened by Roman life, Stoic independence might seem very beautiful, and even the paradoxes that only the wise man is sane and free, not so laughable as before. And yet, however urgently Horace summons himself and others to the pursuit of wisdom, he never isolates *verum* from *decens* for very long; for while it is proper for men of all ages and conditions to study philosophy, no one collection of doctrines, Stoic or other, will be found relevant to every situation and right for every person. Furthermore, the will to pursue truth must be accompanied by an understanding of the limitations of human strength and the varieties of human folly. When Horace calls himself an Epicurean pig or fat Phaeacian, or wonders whether rich capitalists are not happier after all, or argues that a limit must be set to virtue itself, he is showing, more or less seriously, that no theoretical system of ethics can do justice to the color and complexity of an individual's life (especially when he is a poet).

The ironic perspective by which philosophy is kept faithful to ordinary life can best be seen in Epistles I, 1, in the recurrent, ambivalent metaphor *ludus*, which means "play" or "school." Like a weary gladiator who leaves his *ludus* to avoid being slaughtered in the arena, Horace puts aside poetry writing and "other childish things," *cetera ludicra*. Afterwards, however, he asserts that it is never too late to seek wisdom, that old men, like children, have their *elementa* or ABC to learn. While Horace retains an adult independence of the "dictation" of philosophical schoolmasters, he appeals to the real wisdom of *pueri ludentes*, children whose playful, sing-song chant (lines 59-60),

> rex eris si recte facies,
> si non facies, non eris

> (Do right, and you will be a king; do
> wrong, and you'll not be anything),

he finds much more sensible than the lesson, "MAKE MONEY, ALWAYS MAKE MONEY," that businessmen regurgitate like schoolboys, "wallets and slates slung under the left arm." To worldly men, the "perpetual student" will always seem ridiculous; but then, the World of Business is ridiculous.

A second ironic metaphor is that of unbalance. What Horace asks of philosophy is moral guidance, but his awareness of life's variety and complexity prevents him from adhering totally to any one system of thought (lines 13-19):

> You might be curious what leadership or hearth
> preserves me. There's no single master from whom
> I take dictation: where the storm sweeps me away,
> there I pay my respects. Now I grow active,
> sinking under the waves of public life, strictly
> keeping the law of Veritable Virtue; now discreetly relapse into the way of Aristippus, the
> master, not the slave of my surroundings.

Philosophical Interlude

The point is reinforced by the arrangement of the Epistles, which, like that of the Odes, emphasizes variety and contrast. Ideas of comfort and duty, asceticism and social ease and fulfillment, are ironically juxtaposed in neighboring Epistles and often within a single poem. Yet if intellectual freedom can be exhilarating, like "swimming without the cork," its other side is an insecurity that would alarm most ordinary men. In Epistles I, 1, Horace's amusement at fluctuating between Stoic involvement in public affairs and Cyrenaic self-interestedness is accompanied by an equal regret at drifting inconsistently, as much after studying philosophy as before. One reason why he defies popular opinion by studying philosophy is, he argues, that the populace runs from one pursuit to another, ignorant and unsatisfied; yet he himself is equally uneasy (lines 94-105):

> When I meet you with an uneven haircut, you notice;
> when my collar's frayed, or my sleeve, you notice.
> When my mind wars with itself, changes its wants
> and wants what it just changed, agitates, wavers,
> feels itself unsuited, tears down, builds, mixes
> materials, *then* you don't notice, or you say it's all
> much ado about nothing: you don't pack me off to
> the doctor or petition the State to put me in the
> care of a Committee, my best of guardians! and still,
> you get indignant at an ill-cut fingernail on the
> hand of your weak, devoted friend.

Horace's feeling that, sailing before the philosophical winds, his life is no better ordered than before, is shown in the references to insanity; it is also shown in the resentment he feels towards his patron, who takes errors of dress more seriously than confusion of mind, and who therefore fails to provide the *tutela*, or spiritual patronage, for which even a mature student of life may sometimes yearn.

The Epistle ends, significantly, with a smile. The Stoic wise man has every advantage—unless he has the sniffles. The joke reasserts decorum, redirecting Horace's thoughts toward Maecenas and society, reassuring them that he is not fatally engrossed in introspection—not Prince Hamlet, nor meant to be. More important, it shows how *verum* must be tempered by *decens*, philosophical analysis by humorous acceptance of things. A gentle smile, not a grimace, will mark the Epistles. Yet the anxiety behind this smile is as real as the stomach trouble for which Horace took Dr. Musa's cold-water treatment during these years; and only by understanding this anxiety and the mental perplexities around which it centers itself—questions about retreat and social involvement and the nature and value of truth itself—can we properly appreciate these Epistles.

II *Dependence on Place*

One symbolic focus of Horace's uncertainties is the Sabine farm to which he "retired" for leisure, contemplation, and peace of mind. There is more to the line (Epistles I, 8, 12),

Romae Tibur amem ventosus, Tibure Romam,

than meets the eye—more than the old temptation of the Country Mouse—for Horace's restlessness has been exasperated, it seems, by the philosophical inquiries that blow him about from one principle of life to another. The old problem of escapism also troubled him. In Epistles I, 11, he advises a certain Bullatius, who has been touring the East, not to succumb to the lure of novelty and become an expatriate unnecessarily; but the most dangerous attraction for Bullatius may be, not some rich "city of Attalus," but the wish to escape from cares in some quiet, remote, even unheard-of place, like Lebedus (lines 7-10):

> "Lebedus you know: a place more god-forsaken
> than Gabii or Fidenae: still I'd love to
> live there, to forget and be forgotten, and
> safe on shore, look at the sea raging."

It is not clear that Bullatius is speaking (the quotation marks are mine).[5] What matters is that Horace sympathizes with his desire, indeed is nostalgic himself for the Lucretian stance of gazing upon stormy waters from the safety of the shore. His recommendation of contentment here and now is as personal and dramatic as in the Odes, and the first person plural is again much more than tactful (lines 22-30):

[112]

> Whatever time Fortune bestows on you, take with
> a grateful hand, and don't put off the pleasant
> things forever: better to say, wherever you
> have been, there you enjoyed living: for if
> reason removes our cares, and planning, not a
> fine view of the sea, then we change altitude,
> not attitude, when we fly overseas (never so busy
> as in free time, by boat, by car we press toward
> the good life). What you require is here, even—
> if you're at ease—at Ulubrae!

All too easily, the Sabine farm could become another Lebedus. Horace always guarded against false sentimentalism; though he lacked Virgil's intimate knowledge of field, tree, and flock, he valued the country for the concrete benefits it provided—for quiet, charming walks, time to read and sleep, simple meals, simple routine, honest conversation. But what if the searchlight of philosophy revealed a desire to hide from the world, a growing dependence on place to furnish the good life? Is the Sabine farm, where Horace retired to seek "what is true and proper," just another addiction that the philosophical man must renounce?

It all depends: that is Horace's answer. Writing in Epistles I, 10 to Aristius Fuscus, an ironist and the kind of friend with whom we dare not take ourselves or our problems too seriously, he argues, passionately and with conscious exaggeration, that the country provides the only good life. Beneath a humorous façade of argument, he justifies his choice on grounds of propriety: earlier, the "honeyed cakes" of the city might have tempted him, but today his bodily and spiritual condition requires greater independence. His present contentment as he writes "behind the crumbling shrine of Vacuna" (Lady Leisure?) or, better, his joy (the last word of Epistles I, 10 is *laetus,* "joyful") constitutes a sufficient guarantee that his choice of "streams and woods and moss-grown rocks" was the correct one.

Epistles I, 14, to a steward, makes the same point. (The addressee is real enough, his temperament, ideas, even diction nicely envisaged and portrayed; but unlike Fuscus, he shares less in Horace's humor than bears its brunt.) Typically, a crucial point is half concealed in a modifying phrase (line 1):

> vilice silvarum et mihi me reddentis agelli. . . .
>
> (Steward of woodlands and the little field
> that gives me back myself. . . .)

The claim is moving. In Epistles I, 7, Horace tells Maecenas in beautiful, nostalgic verses that if he desires him never to leave Rome, he must give back (*reddes,* emphatically repeated) his strong body, dark hair, sweet speech, proper laughter, drinking, and lovemaking: in short, his youth. And in the last parable of that letter, a deluded client begs his patron, *vitae me redde priori*: "Give me back my former life," but also, by a poetic ambiguity, "Give *me* back" (to myself). The country, in Epistles I, 14, cannot perform a miracle, any more than Maecenas; Horace will never be young again; but precisely because he is middle-aged, he finds the city psychologically overwhelming and cannot keep "in touch with himself" except on the farm. The country is blessed because of the state of mind it provides.

Does this constitute dependence on place, a happiness of illusion? It could be. Horace complains because he is detained in the city, the steward complains in the country (lines 12-13, 18-19):

> Fools both of us, unfairly so to blame
> an undeserving place. The mind's at fault
> that flees itself, in vain. . . .
>
> You and I disagree only in gaping
> after different things.

By the absolute standard of detachment from things, *nil admirari,* Horace is at fault like the steward. He thus deserves the Stoic name, *stultus.* By a more humane view, however, his contentment once more justifies his choice. The steward is condemned, not because he longs for the city's taverns and brothels (for taste is relative) but because he will not be satisfied anywhere. When Horace dismisses his request to be transferred with the abrupt command, "Do your own job and like it," the dramatic way in which he cuts off argument shows how he sees his choice of life, as arbitrary yet right. To the Stoic whose voice is so often heard in the Epistles preaching absolute detachment and regularity of life, this may not do. But the philosopher must be reminded, like Malvolio, that he is only a steward. When his criticism infringes on contentment, it may be cut short with the rightness that an arbitrary act or decision often possesses. It is all a question (as Humpty Dumpty says) of who is master.

III   *Freedom and Society*

This mastery over things and systems is confirmed by the way in which Horace juxtaposes contrasting themes. In Epistles I, 14, he praises the country for the simple, free life it offers; in I, 15, reserves the right to self-indulgence while traveling; in I, 16, turns Stoic and demands an inner-directed standard of virtue: men must be truly good, not whitened "pillars of society." And then: I, 17 and I, 18 are full of precepts for would-be courtiers.

If we remember Horace's insistence on tempering *verum* with *decens,* his advice to Scaeva in I, 17 and Lollius in I, 18 will be less surprising. Simplicity, retirement, country: these are right for Horace now. Rome is full of *officia,* obligations that drain his energies now and encumber his mind; it is not on that account wrong for aspiring youths. In the philosophic puppet play with which I, 7 begins, Diogenes, the Cynic beggar, represents the unencumbered life, free, it would seem, from material possessions and social responsibilities, while Aristippus of Cyrene states the case for what Montaigne later called "the school of dealing with men" (the key phrase, *maioribus uti,* means either "managing a larger property" or "getting on with important people"). Aristippus traditionally won the argument. It is better, he sensibly joked, to "manage kings" than to "manage with vegetables," better to play the fool for oneself than for the mob. And seriously, Horace gives judgment for him (lines 23-42):

> All states, tones, levels suited Aristippus. He
> tried greatness, but took whatever came. Diogenes,
> though, dressed in his tailored rags, won't be
> suited if the roles are reversed. The one's not
> lost without his purple mantle: he'll wear what-
> ever's there, march through the streets, play any
> part you want and not look foolish. But beatnik
> D: there's nothing he hates worse than decent
> clothes; he'll die of cold unless you give his
> rags back. Let him live, a fool.

> He who conducts affairs and wins great triumphs
> touches the throne of Jove, rises to heaven; he
> who could please the great does not come last.
> Not every man, they say, can go to Corinth; some
> stayed, for fear of failure. Let them sit: what
> of those who succeed? Are they real men? That's
> the crux of the matter. One shrinks back, "the
> burden's much too big for his poor mind and frame";
> another undertakes the job, carries it through. If
> virtue's anything, doesn't the man of action rightly
> take the glory and the prize?

Aristippus wins by the standard of decorum. He is more adaptable (*aptus*), can act different parts assigned by fortune with greater versatility and grace. The other is *ineptus*: unfit, tactless, foolish. Aristippus' follower will enjoy luxury, here symbolized by Corinth; he will attain a certain eminence by living agreeably with great men, as Horace has; and by not taking shelter behind the excuse of "smallness" (significantly, a frequent Horatian pose), he will show himself a man.

The debate would seem conclusive. The life of social involvement wins by every criterion: decorum, control, self-fulfillment through activity. Yet the second part of the epistle apparently contradicts the first. Here, by an abrupt plunge into Roman practice, the "kings" of the debate become real Roman patrons, off whom their clients parasitically feed. Horace's precepts to Scaeva are cynical. Don't ask, and you will get more to eat. Don't complain too much, or your patron will become bored. "A beggar pretended to be crippled, he fooled many people. Finally he really broke his leg. And the more he cried and screamed for help, the more his audience laughed: 'Tell it to a stranger,' they said." On this note of cruel, disillusioned laughter the epistle suddenly ends.

As though in reaction to I, 17, I, 18 presents a young man who will not connive or flatter. Lollius will speak his mind, regardless ... but Horace warns him against an excessive, inept frankness. There is an Aristotelian mean, of honest but polite speech, between the extremes of flattery and boorishness. Lollius should not be a yes-man, echoing a patron's words as schoolboys recite their lesson, but neither should he pride himself on ill-mannered speech or uncouth appearance. True freedom is a quality of the soul. It does not depend on rough language or dirty fingernails.

Philosophical Interlude

But another shift of mood and thought follows. In theory, the
mean in conduct is easily comprehended, but real society is full
of pitfalls: one false step and you are ruined. If you live extravagantly, for example, your patron will resent it (folly and vice are
his privilege). Whether you let secrets out, or covet someone's
pretty maidservant, or recommend an undeserving man, ruination
is always near; for (in sum) only fools and young men rush in
where Horace has learned to tread warily (lines 86-87):

> dulcis inexpertis cultura potentis amici,
> expertus metuit.

> (Youth hurries in to cultivate Great Friends:
> once bitten, though, twice shy.)

Similarly, the parables in Epistles I, 7 of the Calabrian host who
forces worthless gifts upon his departing guests, the fox stuck
(rather like Pooh) in a grain bin, and the plebeian Mena whose
health and happiness are ruined when, through his patron's
thoughtlessness, he becomes stuck in a bad situation, all show, at
the distance satire grants, what an abyss of slavishness, resentment,
and hatred yawns beneath the patron-client relationship. Here we
are, Horace seems to say, but for your forbearance and generosity,
Maecenas, and my own affection and gratitude.[6] The *but for* is
crucial. Horace's relation with Maecenas could easily have soured,
yet humor and kindliness keep control. Perhaps, then, the problems confronting Lollius are not insuperable (but perhaps we have
been seeing them through a young man's suspicious eyes). Take
a central difficulty, the clash of tastes. You will be asked to hunt,
says Horace, when you feel like writing poetry. Is that really so
terrible? Isn't the writing of poetry, seen in a comic perspective,
as much a form of play (*lusus, nugae*) as hunting? "We all have
our playthings," writes Lady Mary Wortley Montagu to her
daughter; "happy are those who can be contented with those they
can obtain."[7] And Dr. Johnson argues, somewhat against his inclination, that dinner parties with no worthwhile conversation
can still "promote kindness" and that card playing somewhat
"generates kindness and consolidates society."[8] So too in Rome:
the Muse must not be allowed to turn "dull and inhuman" (*in-
humanae senium Camenae*). Horace ought to know.

And yet (Horace's mind has been moving antithetically) the fact remains that true liberty, however much we clarify and internalize it, can still be intimidated by social pressures. A dismal last warning to Lollius satirizes the patron's intolerance of men whose taste or temperament differs from his own. Is the struggle worth it? Once more, it all depends (lines 96-103):

> Amidst all this, read and consult the wise
> how most smoothly to pass your span of life:
> must your desires always spin you about, or
> fears, or hopes of hardly useful things? Is
> virtue learned, or is it born within us?
> What lessens care? Endears you to yourself?
> What soothes the soul, honor or sweet profits
> or the withdrawn path and the hidden life?

What Horace apparently starts to say is that Lollius must recollect himself in the midst of things. He must retreat, not to some external refuge (for well-being should not depend on place) but into himself. Yet in the samples of meditation here suggested Horace's imagination swings to solitude, as if in reaction to the social pressures and difficulties enumerated earlier. Perhaps Epicurus was right after all, and tranquility exists only in the "hidden life."

Certainly, Horace's present contentment, the final self-assurance with which he asks Jove for a steady supply of food and books but says he will see to his own equanimity, cannot be separated from the particular refreshment made possible by the Sabine farm (line 104):

> me quotiens reficit gelidus Digentia rivus....
>
> (Now every time Digentia's icy stream
> makes me all fresh again....)

Young Lollius will run his race not without dust and heat. Whether his choice is right, or founded on right motives, is uncertain: Lollius will know more after he has ripened, like Horace, in social experience. But one thing is certain. No sensitive spirit can satisfy the demands of society without some inner "Sabine" landscape into which he may retreat at will and from which he may emerge again, refreshed.

IV   *Cheerful Disillusionment*

From Book I of the Epistles, which was published in 20 B.C. with a joking epilogue, we can see that Horace was attracted to philosophy because it promised to simplify his life, concentrate him in purpose, and so establish his independence of things on a sure foundation. But after the simplifications of Stoic and other philosophies have been qualified by a humorous awareness of the complexity of men and society and a feeling that happiness, however won, must take precedence over abstract rules of conduct, what exactly is left of philosophy? Or put differently: what did Horace gain from pursuing *verum atque decens* that he never had before?

The question is raised in Epistles II, 2, to Florus (19 or 18 B.C.). Horace has just explained with his usual irony why he is not writing lyric poems: like Lucullus' soldier, he has no incentive to "re-enlist"; poetry writing is hard; and who can write amid the distractions of Rome? Then he tells a parable (lines 128-40):

> There was, one time, a gentleman of Argos who used
> (he thought) to watch wondrous performers, sat,
> laughed, and clapped—all in an empty theater.
> Otherwise, he was perfectly well adjusted: nice
> to his neighbors, amiable with friends, sweet to his
> wife—he could pardon his slaves and not go mad over
> the *cork au vin*—watched out for rocks, avoided
> gaping holes. But when, by his relations' care and
> wealth, his brain was washed (hemlock served as a kind
> of shock treatment), and he came to himself, "You've
> killed me, people, not delivered me," he said, "my
> greatest treat's taken away, the trick of mind that
> once made me so happy."

The Argive is a Dickensian figure. His eccentricity was harmless, and it helped him fulfill the normal obligations of life with unusual kindness and good will—unlike the rest of us who, being fully awake to reality, are unkind to neighbors, unpleasant to friends, horrid to wives, and tyrannical with servants, "going mad" over an injury to the cork of a wine bottle. What was gained by destroying his illusion?

In its immediate context, the story bears on Horace's attitude toward writing lyric poetry. Just before, he asserted that to write well a man must work hard and accept stringent criticism, and remarked that in such matters, ignorance is bliss (lines 126-28):

> I'd rather seem a crazy, lazy writer, while I
> enjoyed my faults, or else ignored them, than
> have good taste—and bad temper.

The irony partly reinforces Horace's conviction that, since poetry is a high vocation and a chief civilizing force, the mutual admiration societies of poets are not just ridiculous and irritating, but downright harmful. But the point is not merely that it is more comfortable to sleep, physically or at least mentally, than to exert every faculty. It is rather (as *sapere* implies, meaning both "taste" and "sense") that the requirements of good poetry include a deeper clarification of things, a consciousness and sanity imposed by life itself and strengthened by philosophy. When Horace writes (lines 141-44),

> nimirum sapere est abiectis utile nugis,
> et tempestivum pueris concedere ludum,
> ac non verba sequi fidibus modulanda Latinis,
> sed verae numerosque modosque ediscere vitae.

> (Surely sense is useful, bidding us do away
> with trifling and give over to youth their time of play,
> not harmonize fine words upon our Latin strings
> but learn what rhythm Nature sets in the heart of things.)

he is speaking less of abandoning lyric poetry than of renouncing a too playful attitude towards life. Philosophy brings disillusionment, like the brainwashing forced upon the poor Argive. Coming therefore, immediately after the parable, Horace's injunction takes on, especially in *nimirum*, a bitter and sarcastic meaning. Why, after all, should we throw away playthings, yield to youth, and learn the measures and rhythms of right living?

Vanity of vanities, all is vanity—including poetry writing, including even philosophy. For a moment Horace seems to look into the abyss. Then he steps back and returns to his customary role as spokesman, not for the Absurd, but for education, culture, and sanity.

Although *sapere* is always painful, and sometimes overwhelming, yet a relative grasp of *verum atque decens* affords the only enduring foundation of equanimity and the enjoyment of life. The mellow, impersonal second part of Epistles II, 2 shows, even more in tone than assertion, that the study of philosophy can bring, indeed *has brought*, real benefits. By reflecting on the transience of our possessions, we learn to value them rightly and "possess" them most truly. More important: we learn through study to realize and to accept our own mortality.

The question is, not whether we should study philosophy, but whether we have studied it enough. The epistle ends with a spiritual examination, of the kind for which (as someone said of the Last Judgment) no cramming is possible. Like a physician, the philosopher probes for weaknesses. Does the patient suffer from avarice, ambition, superstition? Or (a Horatian touch) from ingratitude and sourness (lines 210-11)?

> natalis grate numeras? ignoscis amicis?
> lenior et melior fis accedente senecta?
>
> (Do you celebrate birthdays? Pardon friends?
> Grow more mellow as every decade ends?)

A man should age well, like good wine. Bad humor is the worst of sins, and sometimes the educator and moralist may turn sour first. The extraordinary thing is that Horace, unlike the Argive, has been able to combine disillusionment with cheerfulness, steadying himself to obey the impersonal and absolute decree of wisdom and politeness (lines 213-16):

> vivere si recte nescis, decede peritis.
> lusisti satis, edisti satis atque bibisti:
> tempus abire tibi est, ne potum largius aequo
> rideat et pulset lasciva decentius aetas.
>
> (If you cannot live well, give way to those who can.
> You've played, eaten, and drunk enough for any man:
> it's time now to depart, unlike those drunken bores
> that young men, who more fittingly sport, kick out
> of doors.)

without relinquishing that quality of good humor which is, in Dr. Johnson's definition, *"a Habit of being pleased,* a constant and perennial Softness of Manner, Easiness of Approach, and Suavity of Disposition."

It is not enough, then, to say that Horace was born cheerful and remained so. His unusual power to enjoy nature, society, and the present moment, was unusually threatened too: by bodily sickness, by psychological discontent and indecision, by an oppressive sense of drifting without purpose in a meaningless universe. What he finally gained and shares with us through his poetry is the final serenity to which those men are entitled who have rightly matured, known joy and sorrow, and—in the broadest sense of the word—studied philosophy.

CHAPTER 7

Indian Summer[1]

I *Acceptance of Growing Old*

AFTER the philosophical epistles, the fourth book of Horace's odes should surprise us. For him to emerge from the retirement in which he forswore all "playthings" to devote himself to philosophy is, in his own terms, highly indecent. Suetonius tells us, to be sure, that Augustus "compelled" him to write Odes IV, 4 and 14, on the victories of Drusus and Tiberius; but this only means that Augustus suggested what Horace was inclined to do (as he had been ready, in 17 B.C., to write a festal hymn for the Secular Games). It does not explain Book IV.

The personality that greets us in these odes is unfamiliar, like an old friend met after a lapse of years. We must adjust our minds. First of all, he is now successful, a "poet laureate" whose work has received official recognition and is acclaimed by the coming generation. It has been fashionable, since Chekhov's plays and Ibsen's, to denigrate success, to contrast its impotent bitterness with the unshaped but idealistic ambitions of unsuccessful beginners; but the generous concern of elder statesmen like Horace, and in our time, Eliot, for younger, aspiring poets gives the lie to that stereotype. Horace was indeed pleased by success, but his pleasure is magnanimous, like that of Wagner's noble Meistersinger, Hans Sachs. Second (but the two go together), Horace tends now more easily to voice the sentiments of the community: his own concerns are unobtrusive or merge with those of Rome; no tension remains between public and private. Yet an integral connection can be perceived between this Horace and the earlier one, and between the impersonal public odes of Book IV and the philosophical epistles; for if the dominant theme of natural process, birth, and right growth and death, gives unity to Book IV, its odes are also bound together in a deeper way by Horace's fairly steady and controlled attitude of acceptance, toward which he fought his way, through paradox and disillusionment, on the Sabine farm.

What is remarkable is that this hard-won calm should be joined with a resurgence of spirit, a renewal of the lyric impulse. But this resurgence should not be mistaken for rebellion, even in Odes IV, 1, where "falling in love" again stands also for returning to lyric poetry (lines 1-8):

> Intermissa, Venus, diu
> rursus bella moves? parce precor, precor.
>   non sum qualis eram bonae
> sub regno Cinarae. . . .
>
> (Venus, our truce was long: now is it
> war again? Spare me: I'm not the man I was
>   when good Cinara reigned. . . .)

Once drinking, lovemaking, and writing lyrics were "appropriate" to Horace's years and temperament: now they are not, so Venus is referred to a young and ardent substitute who will more suitably serve her (*tempestivius, iecur idoneum, decens*). And thereby, with fine indirection, Horace dedicates his book to Paullus Fabius Maximus, one of the group of young aristocrats that Augustus was beginning to associate with himself in the work of government; and through him, to the younger generation, who will inherit the reins of politics, poetry—and living. We shall see how Horace's concern for youth pervades Book IV. He genuinely wishes to get out of their way gracefully. And yet, as Emerson said, "Nature is full of freaks, and now puts an old head on young shoulders, and then a young heart beating under fourscore years."[2] As Horace (only fifty-two) knew from the first, his plea was bound to fail; and so it does (lines 29-40):

> me nec femina nec puer
> iam nec spes animi credula mutui
>   nec certare iuvat mero
> nec vincire novis tempora floribus.
>   sed cur heu, Ligurine, cur
> manat rara meas lacrima per genas?
>   cur facunda parum decoro
> inter verba cadit lingua silentio?

> nocturnis ego somniis
> iam captum teneo, iam volucrem sequor
> te per gramina Martii
> campi, te per aquas, dure, volubilis.

> (No girl I choose, nor boy; expect no mutual
> bond of love; relish no drinking bouts; bind
> my forehead with no fresh flowers. But why,
> Ligurinus, why does a tear steal down my cheek?
> Why that eloquent tongue in mid-speech fall shame-
> fully dumb? Yes: in my dreams at night I hold
> you now, now pursue you swiftly over the fields
> or, callous boy, through rapid waters.)

It is a beautiful ending. The situation is common: a man tries to overcome love by reason, but love wins out. Thus, in a poem of Theocritus, a man falls in love with a beautiful youth: he rebukes his spirit for its improper suggestion (improper because he is too old), but his spirit replies that love is irresistible.[3] Just so, dramatically and with beautiful self-irony (notice the play on *decorum* and *cor*) Horace reveals that his heart is vulnerable after all. The sexual imagery of the last verses shows the power of the unconscious to surprise us with a flood of unsuspected feeling. We should not, however, read Odes IV, 1 as a Romantic rejection of the sane and orderly outlook to which the terms of "propriety" point. Horace's poem differs altogether from Mann's story "Death in Venice," where the same metaphor, of an aging writer's love for a beautiful boy, shows the destructive side of art, neglected nature's vengeance on the Apollinian artist. The maleness of Ligurinus is irrelevant; homosexual love does not imply decadence, any more than in Greek lyric poetry. The strength of feeling is what counts. But again, we should not read the poem with too much pathos. Horace is not pleading for passion over reason. His is not the irony of Yeats's later poems, like "Men Improve with the Years," which savagely belies its title. Probably Catullus, had he lived to fifty, would have been an unreconstructed Romantic like Yeats. Horace was never a Romantic to begin with. Unlike Frost (another unreconstructed Romantic?), whom Commager quotes, he is fully able to "bow and accept the end/of a love or a season."[4] He is only a rebel insofar as living is an instinctive rebellion against dying. His tears pay tribute to feeling without denying self-control; their sadness springs less from the pangs, perhaps quite imaginary, of unrequited love than from a deep-seated awareness of mortality. But let us make no mistake: they are also tears of joy, at the Indian summer of his creativity. Not Yeats nor Frost, but Eliot has perhaps best shown in our century this rare combination of the resigned and accepting heart and the renewal of poetic, even youthful feeling.

Indeed, the sequence Odes IV, 10-13 shows how little bitterness or resentment Horace feels toward time. The first of these is a prophecy to Ligurinus that grown old (like Horace), he will complain (lines 7-8):

> quae mens est hodie, cur eadem non puero fuit,
> vel cur his animis incolumes non redeunt genae?
>
> (I should have known, when I was gay and young,
> what time has later taught: wisdom is much too
> dearly bought if now my beard won't go away.)

The arrogant youth here represents the common human tendency, not to live in the present. Those who have grasped the present need not complain. Thus the following poem, as it describes Horace himself as an aging lover, is surely, as Fraenkel has said, "all gentleness and mellow resignation."[5] From the evocation of a wine jar which (like the poet) has improved with the years, to the central celebratory mention of Maecenas' birthday, to a symbolic farewell to the "last of my loves," the ode is unified by the theme of transience and the spirit of acceptance. Symbolically, Phyllis is not for him. Like Hans Sachs, again, he exercises forbearance: the two will be joined together in music, not love. Yet while their innocent relation is meant to amuse us ("Say I'm growing old, but add, Jenny kissed me"), it also illustrates Horace's wisdom, his nongrasping enjoyment of life.[6] He can observe limit, unlike Phaeton and Bellerophon, and still be happy, albeit in a way bordering on melancholy.

The same quiet acceptance can be seen in the next ode, IV, 12.

> Iam veris comites, quae mare temperant,
> impellunt animae lintea Thraciae;
> iam nec prata rigent nec fluvii strepunt
>   hiberna nive turgidi.

nidum ponit Ityn flebiliter gemens
infelix avis et Cecropiae domus
aeternum opprobrium, quod male barbaras
    regum est ulta libidines.

dicunt in tenero gramine pinguium
custodes ovium carmina fistula
delectantque deum cui pecus et nigri
    colles Arcadiae placent.

adduxere sitim tempora, Vergili;
sed pressum Calibus ducere Liberum
si gestis, iuvenum nobilium cliens,
    nardo vina merebere.

nardi parvus onyx eliciet cadum,
quae nunc Sulpiciis accubat horreis,
spes donare novas largus amaraque
    curarum eluere efficax.

ad quae si properas gaudia, cum tua
velox merce veni: non ego te meis
immunem meditor tingere poculis,
    plena dives ut in domo.

verum pone moras et studium lucri,
nigrorumque memor, dum licet, ignium
misce stultitiam consiliis brevem:
    dulce est desipere in loco.

(Now spring's companions, the winds of
Thrace, quiet the sea for navigation:
meadows unstiffen, streams run free, no
longer swollen with ice. For Itys' tear-
ful mother it's time to build her nest—
the unhappy bird and eternal shame of
Athens, who took such a foul revenge. Now
shepherds watching their sheep sit down on
delicate grass, and play on pipes songs
rejoicing the heart of Pan, dark Arcadia's god.

The season makes us thirsty, Virgil. If
you want wine from Cales' vineyards, patron of noble lords, you'll have it in exchange for ointment. See, a small ointment

box will entice into your arms most excellent wine, bringing great projects, liqui-
dating despondency and care. If these delights
tempt you, then hurry, but bring your merch-
andise: I'm not thinking of letting you soak
yourself scot-free; I'm not that rich, you
know.

But really, put your business aside,
and, mindful of the funeral pyre, mix
some folly with wisdom; there are moments
to play the fool.)

This "Virgil" (Vergilius) is not the poet, dead several years now,[7]
but a less intimate friend, a businessman with whom Horace jokes
in terms of his profession, as he did with the lawyer Torquatus in
Epistles I, 5. The lesson, that Vergilius must relax and "mix the
wine" of life properly, is familiar: we saw it in Odes II, 3 and II,
11; but here, despite the nudge of *dum licet*, no vehement personal urgency contradicts the lesson given. Death's dark fires are
here, but the "dark hills" of Arcadia, anticipating them, are an
image of natural beauty and serenity. The gentle melancholy induced by thoughts of death is natural and need not disturb our
calm, any more than walking through a cypress-laden cemetery.
The Asclepiadic meter, too, has a soothing effect, unlike the Alcaic. Its even rhythm, like the wine, which will not "dispel" cares
but (literally) "wash out the bitterness," points to the healing
relaxation of spirit of which Vergilius is invited to partake.

Yet while the addressee is an ordinary man, Horace is also thinking of Virgil, the "half of his soul." Right out of the Eclogues are
these shepherds' pipes that inspire joy. In many ways, too, the ode
recalls I, 24, on Quintilius' death. The meter is the same. The
word *flebiliter* and the placing of *Vergili* recall

nulli flebilior quam tibi, Vergili,

and the word play, *veris—Vergili—verum*, recalls that of *Veritas/
Vergili*. We may go further. As Professor Edwin Brown has
shown, Virgil plays on his own name, Publius Vergilius Maro, in
Georgics I and II; among other associations, he joins *Vergilius*

with *ver*, "spring."[8] When Horace, therefore, changes the opening of Catullus' spring poem, 46,

> iam ver egelidos refert tepores,

to his own

> iam veris comites . . .,

he is recalling his intimacy with Virgil and also making a significant contrast. Catullus ended his poem with a sentimental farewell to his companions (*comites*); but Horace, just as he enjoys the refreshment of a new spring (*ver*), has learned to enjoy the Virgilian spirit of pastoral serenity by which even sadness at death—even Virgil's death—may be contained. The swallow bewails her lost child, but her song is part of nature's sweetness, and while she sings, she builds her nest. So, despite their sadness, Horace and Vergilius (who may be a relative of the poet) are most truly *veris comites*, sharers even now in Virgil's spirit, when they participate in the easing of spring. Elsewhere, in Odes IV, 7, for example, Horace contrasts the seasons' renewal with man's linear movement toward a single death. But in Odes IV, 12, man's spirit is resurrected like the spring itself.

Humor is a great part of the pastoral spirit, and I have made IV, 12 more solemn than Horace intended it. His wish is not so much to jolt Vergilius into mindfulness of the "black fires" as to tease him into relaxation and a right mixture of life, such as he himself has learned to mix and drink.

Notice that the ending gives no incitement to riot or rebellion. Folly must be brief and in place. So controlled, it is part of life's wisdom, of the right "mixture" that Horace embodies and recommends; but carried further, it is very ugly. In Odes IV, 13, Horace describes an aging courtesan who will not yield to youth and beauty. Once she was beautiful: and Horace's memories of her youth and his blaze up in memorable verses; but now, his old flame is "reduced to ashes." It is her clinging to the past that makes her an object of derision. She is the counterpart of Ligurinus in IV, 10, who behaves as though his charms will last forever, but her folly is less pardonable than his. Horace mocks her, not from revenge but because her resistance to nature's law is so very ugly—

and because there but for the grace of wisdom goes the poet himself. His own acceptance of time, felt behind Odes IV, 11 and IV, 12, is framed by the more satirical and objective poems, IV, 10 and 13, on beauty youthful and decayed.

II   *Roman Continuity and Growth*

By recognizing the importance of gratitude in Horace's late writings, we avoid the mistaken idea that he regarded the power of poetry negatively, as a compensation for mortality. A superficial reading of Odes IV, 7-9 would encourage such a view. In IV, 7, which is extremely beautiful, man's linear movement toward a single death is contrasted with nature's cyclic continuity, her power of renewal and rebirth (lines 13-16):

> damna tamen celeres reparant caelestia lunae:
>   nos ubi decidimus
> quo pater Aeneas, quo Tullus dives et Ancus,
>   pulvis et umbra sumus.

> (Moons of heaven swiftly repair
> their losses in the upper air,
>   but when we mortals fall
> where Tullus, Ancus, and the best
> of men, Aeneas, came to rest,
>   we are nothing at all.)

The mood is elegiac. While the meter, dactylic hexameters followed by half-pentameters, reinforces the contrast between nature's continuity and man's abrupt end, the regular over-all rhythm expresses not urgency nor flight but a quiet, melancholy certainty. There is no rebellion here against reason, conveyed through imagery or sound or dramatic structure, as in Odes II, 3 and II, 11. Yet if Odes IV, 7 scarcely grasps at life, Odes IV, 8 and 9, on the power of poetry, gain effect from its backdrop of mortality. In IV, 8, poetry, more than likenesses in bronze, restores the "breath of life" after death; without it, heroic efforts would go unrewarded (lines 25-30):

> ereptum Stygiis fluctibus Aeacum
> virtus et favor et lingua potentium
> vatum divitibus consecrat insulis.

> dignum laude virum Musa vetat mori:
> caelo Musa beat. sic Iovis interest
> optatis epulis impiger Hercules....

> (From Stygian waves Aeacus was wrested by
> excellence and grace and the strong voice
> of poets to abide in the Rich Islands:
> the Muse forbids deserving souls to die,
> the Muse grants heaven. Only so is mighty
> Hercules seated at the feast of Jove....)

Isn't this going rather far, to say that the rewards traditionally attributed to heroes are realized only through poetry? And again in IV, 9, when Horace tells Lollius that many poetic forms, including lyric, can confer immortality, and adds (lines 25-28),

> vixere fortes ante Agamemnona
> multi: sed omnes illacrimabiles
> urgentur ignotique longa
> nocte, carent quia vate sacro...

> (Many heroes lived before Agamemnon:
> all are unknown, unwept, overwhelmed
> in death's long night. No sacred poet
> bade them live...)

doesn't this pathos—almost a kind of blackmail—contradict the Stoic theme illustrated in the second half of the poem, that the wise man is self-sufficient and happy?

Certainly, Horace wishes to stimulate Lollius to praiseworthy deeds and is not above using the death's head as a prod. Yet Lollius, like Censorinus in IV, 8, is relatively unimportant: the poems are about the more general and lasting relation of poetry to human excellence. Indeed, the word *favor* points back to the Greek *Kharis*, which in Pindar's epinician odes has four interrelated meanings. First, the *Kharites* (Horace's *Gratiae*, who dance in IV, 7) preside over the spirit of feasts and celebrations, gracing those rare and happy moments when life seems illuminated with meaning. Second, *Kharis* stands for the corresponding gleam in poetry as the poet responds to a brilliant action and to the generosity of his patron, who has invited him to commemorate it. Third, *Kharis* represents a generous and grateful outlook that endures through disappointment. This is well expressed in *Pythian 2*, where despite recent misunderstandings Pindar attests his fundamental loyalty to Hieron, his gratitude for past kindnesses and deeds of excellence.[9] But fourth, in this very gratitude, this refusal to "batten on hatred," Pindar displays that awareness of human limit of which the gods approve and on which genuine success must ultimately depend. The myth of Ixion related in *Pythian 2*, like the stories of Coronis, Tantalus, and Bellerophon, shows how sin and self-destruction are rooted in an attitude of nonacceptance, a striving for more than is right. That way lies folly—the infatuation of mind shown in Ixion's sleeping with a cloud—and utter ruin.

When Horace then writes

> virtus et favor et lingua potentium
> vatum,

he is thinking not of a poet's lobby, but of poetry as a response to excellence; but this response is connected, as in Pindar, with the poet's own grateful acceptance of life. We saw earlier how Horace reinterpreted the Greek ideal of *sôphrosynê*, or "safe-wittedness"; how classical balance and restraint were threatened for him as well as enforced by mortality; and how he attempted to secure for himself an enduring, philosophical attitude toward living and dying. Yet perhaps the chief lesson the philosophers taught had been anticipated by Pindar's spirit of *Kharis*, which Horace now came most fully to understand and recreate.

To his private acceptance of things, two prominent themes of his most public poetry are closely related: the continuity of the generations and the importance of right growth. These appear already in the *Carmen Saeculare*, written at Augustus' request in 17 B.C. The Secular Games, whose meaning the ode was to celebrate, had always included propitiation of the nether gods by sacrifice and prayer; but Augustus' new emphasis on the Fates, the Birth Goddess, Mother Earth in her aspect of fertility, and the gods of light (especially Apollo and Diana), seems in its concentration on birth and right growth to have struck a responsive chord in Horace's imagination. Here was another and a greater Anniversary to be thankful for. When the poet appeals to the Birth Goddess to "carry on the race" and foster marriage laws, he is concerned with *propaganda* in the root sense. The *leges Iuliae* will make Italy fruitful. They will ensure what matters most: that—long after Horace is dead—this joyful occasion may again be renewed.

If Horace's feeling for the occasion is Pindaric, his longer view owes much to Virgil. The allusions in the *Carmen Saeculare* to Aeneas' travels, from burning Troy, over seas, to Italy, show the strong impression made on him by Virgil's historical vision, the pattern of destruction and creation he perceived. Horace too fuses Augustus with Aeneas (lines 49-52):

> quaeque vos bobus veneratur albis,
> clarus Anchisae Venerisque sanguis,
> impetret, bellante prior, iacentem
> lenis in hostem.

> (White oxen slain, grant the request Venus'
> and Anchises' scion makes in prayer, a
> victor who shows pity for the vanquished.)

Many scholars have pointed to the origin in Aeneid VI, 851-53, of the moral demand here placed on Augustus, to win wars but show forbearance afterwards. The suppliant's posture is more significant. By sacrificing white oxen, Augustus will propitiate the gods; but his posture also implies the inner wisdom and self-sacrifice that Aeneas learns, especially in Aeneid VI and VIII. Whether in Virgil's poem, in the Secular Games, or on the great Altar of Peace, this spirit of sacrifice guarantees the continuity of peace and prosperity for which Horace's choir of youths and maidens prays.

Despite its formal requirements, the *Carmen Saeculare* does not differ in spirit from later odes. Consider IV, 6, which has been thought to owe a formal, external unity to Pindar's sixth Paean. Here, as there, Apollo is god of bow and lyre, and Horace turns like Pindar from mythic narrative to his official chorus. But another connection is deeper and more Pindaric. Apollo's might was shown in his causing Achilles' death, but this was required by the growth of Rome (lines 17-24):

> sed palam captis gravis, heu nefas, heu
> nescios fari pueros Achivis
> ureret flammis, etiam latentem
> matris in alvo,

ni tuis victus Venerisque gratae
vocibus divum pater adnuisset
rebus Aeneae potiore ductos
alite muros. . . .

(*He'd* have attacked more openly, roasted
the infant babes of Troy in Greek camp-
fires, even those hid in their mother's
womb, had not the father of gods, compelled
by your prayers and by Venus' grace, granted Aeneas walls to build under a better sign.)

Imagery and idea go back to the Aeneid, to the Trojan horse with
its hidden destructive progeny, and the emergence of Rome from
a secret seed carried from Troy and replanted in Italian soil. But
this birth of the future was precisely what the choir had prayed
for. The god of song and historical growth are one, but so is Horace in his private feelings and his public role, as the ending confirms (lines 41-44):

nupta iam dices "ego dis amicum,
saeculo festas referente luces,
reddidi carmen docilis modorum
vatis Horati."

(Married, you'll say: "*I* was one who
sang the Anniversary hymn, never miss-
ing the even beat set by the seer,
Horace.")

This is no mere *sphragis,* or signature. It recalls the sentimental
ending of Odes II, 6, *vatis amici.* There, Septimius was to weep
over the still glowing ashes of his "poet friend"; but here, Horace's
own death is unimportant: it is enough that one of his young sing-
ers will grow old in marriage, carry on the race, and incidentally
remember this occasion (and Horace) with fond thoughts. They
had celebrated this continuity together and worked and prayed to
further it. Horace can be grateful for the future he will not live
to see.

The fusion of personal feeling and public concern and of Pindaric and Virgilian themes of time, growth, and history, can again
be seen in Odes IV, 4, which celebrates the victory of Drusus and

Tiberius over the Raetians and which, of all Horace's odes except the *Carmen Saeculare*, gives the strongest impression of having been written to order. It is another work of propaganda in the root sense, a meditation, ostensibly on victory, but more essentially on personal and historical growth. Augustus' stepsons first elicit our sympathy not as conquerors but as young, growing eaglets. The present victory confirms their physical and moral excellence (lines 25-36):

> ... sensere, quid mens rite, quid indoles
>   nutrita faustis sub penetralibus
>   posset, quid Augusti paternus
>   in pueros animus Nerones.
>
> fortes creantur fortibus et bonis;
> est in iuvencis, est in equis patrum
>   virtus, neque imbellem feroces
>   progenerant aquilae columbam:
>
> doctrina sed vim promovet insitam,
> rectique cultus pectora roborant;
>   utcumque defecere mores,
>   indecorant bene nata culpae.

(Then they were struck by what training
mind and character could receive, once
Nero's children enjoyed Augustus' fath-
erly concern. Brave fathers produce brave
offspring: cattle and horses keep the
power their parents had, and the kite
cannot beget a timid dove; but learning
furthers inborn might, and education
steels the heart: when good morals decline, even good birth can meet disgrace.)

Horace tips the scales here against Pindar's *phua,* or inborn nature. Without right direction, aristocratic excellence will fester. But Augustus, who in Odes III, 4 receives the Muses' counsel, now embodies it; Horace has come to trust his judgment and self-restraint, and can therefore see the courage and vigor of the old Roman aristocracy as united now, in Tiberius and Drusus, with the controlling, Augustan wisdom of the new era (somewhat reversing

Odes I, 12, where the betrothal of Marcellus to Augustus' daughter Julia was depicted as a union of slow-growing tree and blazing star). Yet both components of success are joined in a larger *phua*, illustrated by metaphors of grafting and cultivation in the verses quoted above. Body and spirit, a person grows like a tree. And behind the present victory is the slow, right growth of Rome herself, as seen in the older, more ideal victory over Hannibal (who is speaking; lines 53-60):

> gens, quae cremato fortis ab Ilio
> iactata Tuscis aequoribus sacra
> natosque maturosque patres
> pertulit Ausonias ad urbis,
>
> duris ut ilex tonsa bipennibus
> nigrae feraci frondis in Algido,
> per damna, per caedis ab ipso
> ducit opes animumque ferro.

> ("That stock, that from the flames of
> Troy, tossed about on Etruscan waves,
> carried its sons and fathers all the
> way to Italian towns: like an oak shorn
> of many limbs by axe-men on dark Algidus,
> even losses increase it: the very blows
> renew its strength.")

Once more Aeneas, as Virgil depicted him, embodies the Roman spirit; but even more Virgilian than the references to Aeneas' adventures and sufferings is the comparison of the Roman people to a great tree that, being pruned, gains new vigor. Like Virgil, Horace is perfectly aware of the brutality of war. Many animal similes point to it in the present ode. He celebrates the recent victory less as a triumph of civilized order over savagery (although this is there, as in Aeneid VII-XII), than as part of a long, quasi-agricultural process that dwarfs victories—and makes use of defeats. The achievement is gradual, the long range vision is what counts.

What troubles us most about the political odes of Book IV, and especially Odes IV, 5 and IV, 15, both to Augustus, is the absence of inner conflict. Critics have variously argued for Horace's sincerity: by pointing to Horace's familiar, Callimachean refusal to write a long historical poem whose form and content would be alien to his ability and inclination (he will celebrate Augustus' achievements only in his own voice, within his own limits); by relating the ode to earlier poems, whose moral and political demands have now been fulfilled (there are many connecting metaphors); and by stressing Horace's ending and use of the first person plural, and concluding that he speaks not for himself but for the Romans generally—for ordinary people who, being grateful to Augustus for the peace and prosperity they enjoy, praise him as though he were a god.

There is truth in all this, but Horace's sincerity goes deeper. It lies, as ever, in an integration of personal feeling and lyric expression; only what is expressed here is not, as in the Roman Odes, Horace's "quarrel with himself" but an inner sense of agreement. He admires Augustus, to be sure, and even likes him; he is genuinely grateful to him for his work of reconstruction; and once more, he cares deeply about Rome's continuity, its spiritual growth (*crevere*) rooted in tradition, and its renewal through offspring, which he regards as truly his own (*nostris*). But his thanksgiving reflects more than a transient emotion. It rests on his two guiding principles. There is, first, a time for everything: a time to make demands and set conditions, to hold up the ideal as a challenge to the real; and a time to be grateful for actual accomplishments.[10] There is no bitter irony here. Horace may be like the "safe ox" in IV, 5, 17, who "saunters through the countryside,"

> tutus bos etenim rura perambulat,

but he has not sold out for security. Rather (and here is the second principle, related to the first) he accepts reality: accepts the Augustan Age in place of the Golden Age. Now, as never before, he can be satisfied and content.[11] He can also praise Augustus, as never before, for having carried out his mission like the ancient heroes, like Aeneas.

Appropriately, as Horace finds personal fulfillment in the general happiness of the Roman people, speaking at once, as a classical poet may, for himself and for the nation, a symbol borrowed from Virgil marks the completion both of his personal development and his lyric task. Venus is goddess of love in Odes IV, 1 and mother of Aeneas and the Roman race in IV, 15; but since she unites both roles as goddess of creativity—of that cosmic process of which love, poetry, and political growth are each a part—she is for Horace, like Phoebus Apollo, a shining figure of reconciliation and of completion.

III *Cultural Maturation*

In his 1955-56 Harvard lectures entitled "The Estate of Poetry," the poet Edwin Muir contrasted the range and influence once possessed by poetry with its contemporary decline.[12] Although, Muir argued, we need poetry more than ever, to give a true and clear picture of life, it is unlikely to regain its "natural estate," or anything like it, in our increasingly mechanized and fragmented age. Horace's plea in his last epistles is as urgent as Muir's but less pessimistic. It too rests upon a strongly felt contrast, between ideal and reality: the Romans are gifted enough, but their attitude is frivolous and their craftsmanship sloppy; with sense and effort, however, this can be remedied.

In both epistles, II, 3 (the *Ars Poetica*) and II, 1, to Augustus, Horace writes as a critic, not a poet; but the impersonal standards he voices generalize, as they complete, the specific Augustan ambitions to which his own poetry conformed: the desire to extend Hellenistic standards of artistry to great matters, of morality and politics, that had to be treated in the "greater genres." Virgil and Varius had done this in epic, and Horace in lyric (despite all ironies); tragedy remained to conquer. At the same time, these final statements on poetry are, with Odes IV, the culmination of his personal moral formation. To accept the impersonal discipline of good writing is, like the acceptance of growing old, an act of self-abnegation and submission to nature's order: Horace's version, in short, of *pietas*. The demands of poetry are a special instance of the demands of philosophy. In Epistles II, 2, Horace connected the two, but half resisted: wouldn't the self-deluded man be happier? But by Odes IV and Epistles II, 3 and 1, the choice is made, the struggle over that characterized much of Horace's earlier work. His last writings, though full of good humor, are like a testament made in preparation for death.

Although little can be added to the recent work of Becker and Brink on the *Ars Poetica,* it is worth bringing out once more the importance of the themes of time and right growth, with their background in Horace's personal experience. These emerge most clearly in relation to the development of language and the principles of *imitatio* and *decorum*.

In Epistles II, 2, Horace gave the poet a "censorial power" over laguage; in the *Ars*, he justifies the creation of new poetic words by appealing to the general rhythms of nature under which the development of language falls (lines 58-72, esp. 60-63):

> ut silvae foliis pronos mutantur in annos,
> prima cadunt: ita verborum vetus interit aetas,
> et iuvenum ritu florent modo nata vigentque.
> debemur morti nos nostraque....

> (As the years turn, forests are stripped
> of leaves in time of fall: so words grow
> old and die, and new ones come to life,
> flourish and grow. All that we are and
> all we have is mortal.)

The tone is Lucretian. Horace's analogy, with its Homeric comparison of men to leaves, implies his own inward acceptance of the pattern of growth and decay in nature. He asks for new words what in the *Carmen Saeculare* and Odes IV he had asked for Rome: a chance for the future to be born and grow rightly in its turn. Similarly, he asks recognition in Epistles II, 1 not for himself but for a younger generation who must be given a fair chance, not victimized by that envy or hatred of the present that masks itself behind an exaggerated and ridiculous admiration for the earliest Roman writers. Horace has had his place in the sun, now he yields it to the young people.

Of course, loyalty to the past is fully as important as reverence for the future. Old words may be refurbished as well as new ones coined. From his own experience, Horace redefines the classical doctrine of *imitatio*: he wants, not a slavish copying, nor a wild-eyed struggle for originality, but the rooting of poetry in tradition that makes it most fully original and creative, like its models. Young men must not be overwhelmed by past achievements, but they must nourish their inspiration and art on the best Greek *exempla*, in order to translate and renew the life of poetry.

A third, overriding principle closely associated with poetic growth and tradition is *decorum*. This concept (*to prepon* in Greek) was a commonplace of post-Aristotelian rhetorical and poetic theory. It was also, as we saw, a guiding principle of Horace's life. In the *Ars* it leads from specific admonitions concerning style and content to the more fundamental question of right attitude, treated specially in the last part; but it points even in the more technical sections toward a general responsiveness to natural change. Thus when Horace advises the playwright to suit characterization, like diction, to the respective Ages of Man, his descriptive verses (156-76), which, like Shakespeare's, are comprehensive, compassionate, and unprotesting, show that Horace is requiring in drama what he himself did in lyric: an acknowledgment and expression of what change means in human life. But this is part of the larger understanding that must be won from philosophy (lines 306-18):

> Not poetizing now, I'll teach the poet his function
> and the sources of his strength, what's right or
> wrong, successful or mistaken. All good writing
> begins with understanding. For content, see what
> the Socratics write, which once absorbed, good
> style is sure to follow. If a man knows his patri-
> otic duty and debt of love to relatives and friends,
> and knows his obligation in the senate, courtroom,
> or army, he must also know the style befitting every
> character. Let life itself, then, be your primary
> source, if you'd create a dialogue with force.

Notice the stress on duty. Writing poetry is one of many interrelated responsibilities (*munus, officium*) imposed by a life lived in keeping with reality. Yet all this is liberating; for the principle of *decorum*, like that of *imitatio*, is not static but dynamic; the rule is kept relevant to the person and the situation; and *sapere*, like the Socratic *epistêmê*, must be expressed in life as well as explained in theory. The old saying *rem tene, verba sequentur* ("grasp the matter, the words will follow") is both suggestive and misleading: suggestive, because it shows that poetry, like rhetoric, should be grounded in an understanding of real life; and misleading, because this understanding arises out of practical experience and falls back into it, and accordingly, is inseparable from its "stylistic" expression in action or poetry. Horace does not say that to be a good poet one must first (in time) be a good man; no poet would say that. But he feels that the philosophical attitude somehow has primacy.

The pervasive emphasis of the *Ars* on craftsmanship is itself subject to the principle of *decorum*, being relative to the needs of an age that ran to dilettantism. If Horace follows Aristotle's advice in resisting the nearest and most dangerous extreme in his campaign to establish the mean, he nonetheless makes it perfectly clear, by numerous repetitions, that great poetry requires a balance of art and inspiration, hard work and talent, seriousness and play, and has the twofold aim of giving pleasure and instruction. All these inseparable pairs are of course exemplified in the epistle itself, which adapts traditional arrangements of critical precepts to the ironic conversational style of the *sermo*. Yet one thing remains to be accepted without its opposite. This is the sanity and moral order to which art in its fullest meaning points. The alternative is insanity—basically, a refusal to accept nature's law. Indeed, disorderliness of language and disorganization of material are, like eccentricities of dress and appearance, signs of a deeper disorder within. In Epistles II, 2, the "insane man" was a happy and useful eccentric with whom Horace sympathized. In the *Ars*, the mad poet is a grotesque figure possessed by a spirit of rebellion; and as Virgil saw, those who rebel against order must perish in madness. Let them, if they want, says Horace. He might have added (but the ending is negative, in the satiric manner) that a poet may flirt with rebellion long and intensely, but to be a good poet—as to be a good man—he must ultimately align himself on the side of order.

He will thereby serve society. This is a leading idea of Epistles II, 1, to Augustus. The epistle goes beyond the simpler intentions usually attributed to it, such as encouraging Augustus to help contemporary, nontheatrical poets, or reporting on the current state of Roman letters: it describes the poet's relation to his society, which Horace exemplifies (but of course never says so); and by its place of honor—the same as that of Satires II, 1, a social justification of satire—it implies that the poet's role as citizen and teacher is primary. This political emphasis, like the moral in II, 3, is Augustan and Roman, and also classical; and the epistle moves freely between three realms: Augustan culture, Roman culture, and civilization generally.

Horace begins with Augustus, who had in fact requested a *sermo* addressed to himself:

> cum tot sustineas et tanta negotia solus,
> res Italas armis tuteris, moribus ornes,
> legibus emendes, in publica commoda peccem,
> si longo sermone morer tua tempora, Caesar.

> (Since you alone sustain such heavy duties
> that Italy is guarded, graced, and cleansed
> all by yourself, I'd be a public menace if
> I monopolized your notice, Caesar.)

His tact shows genuine respect, a right sense of proportion. Augustus has "undertaken" a Herculean burden; his responsibilities *(negotia)* "deny leisure" to him in order to help others, including poets. Horace also knows, however, that poetry born of leisure is politically responsible in its own way, a civilizing force like law. Augustus will also individually require the services of poetry, to celebrate his excellence in an enduring manner. At the same time, the relation between poet and *princeps* was never one-sided. Poets need recognition and help (thus, the ironic lines 224-28); and we might add, as Horace does not, that political involvement sometimes brings out their greatest possibilities of personal expression. There is always risk. Bad poets write propaganda. But for the *Aeneid* and the Roman Odes Augustus and Maecenas may perhaps, once more, be given their share of credit.

Furthermore, the Augustan culture is a culmination of the Roman. In an apparent excursus, Horace describes the development of Roman drama, as it passed through a stage of excessive *libertas* and was then restrained by law (lines 152-55):

> At last, a legal penalty was found
> to which libelous poets all were bound,
> and they, unwilling to be liable,
> wrote poems more reliable and sound.

As in Satires II, 1, a play on words *(malum carmen/bene dicendum)* brings out the close relation between the writing of good poetry and the acceptance of social responsibility—something Horace had learned from experience. One side of "culture" is literary refinement. The rough countryside of Latin literature required—and still could use—"cultivation" after the best Greek models. On the other side, however, the acceptance of "law" implies a civic consciousness concerning which Greece could learn much from Rome. The best "cultivation," as Horace saw it, required a uniting of the Greek and Roman virtues, which at best are complementary: liberty and law, play and seriousness, flexibility of intellect and solid strength of character. By combining the same seemingly antithetical qualities, the poet will achieve his purpose, "to instruct and to delight."

Poets who like Virgil and Horace realize how thin the fabric of civilization is, are most likely to feel its beauty and be grateful for it. But if poetry is a product of a given culture, it is itself a principal civilizing force, and herein lies its final justification to society. Horace represented Augustus earlier in the epistle as a civilizer, like Hercules with his *labores* (similarly, Virgil connects Hercules, Aeneas, and Augustus). But the poet is his necessary ally. Merely a harmless idiot by one view, he is *utilis urbi*, a civic benefactor, by another (126-38):

> The poet shapes the tender lips of youth
> and turns its ear to decency and truth;
> his soft instruction so informs the mind
> that malice fades and roughness is refined.
> Good actions he recalls, rears the new age
> by bringing old examples on the stage,
> consoles the poor, encourages the weak.
> How could our boys and maidens learn to speak
> suitable prayers, without a poet's care?
> The chorus prays, and knows the gods are there:
> with rightful words it seeks their help again,
> averts disease, and sweetly calls for rain;
> and they, both high and low, to verse give ear
> and grant a peaceful and prosperous year.

The sequence of thought has autobiographical implications, for Horace's own path led from *obsceni sermones* (cf. Satires I, 2) to the *Carmen Saeculare*, sung by innocent boys and girls in an old

religious tradition. Once achieved, however, this personal development is rightly kept in the background. As in Odes IV, what
Horace wants is rather to be instrumental in the right growth and
continuity of the race. Like Augustus, Virgil, and Livy, he "recalls" the heroic actions of the past for the benefit of the future, the
"rising years" and coming generation who must be educated rightly and civilized into manhood. This idea of the poet as guide and
teacher of his people is classical. It went out with the Greek *polis*:
now Augustus and the poets have cooperated in making it once
more a reality, and one that will endure, though variously transformed, long after Virgil and Horace become the Ancients in their
turn.

Professor Klingner has pointed out the irony of the situation.
Horace already belonged to a literary past; the young authors for
whose rights he was pleading were already writing poems foreign
to his taste and inclination; and if the epistle shows Horace's "faith
in the necessity of building further on ground already won," it
still is "the last word of the great Augustan poetry."[13] The irony
is indeed striking. With Ovid, the Golden Age of Latin literature
becomes gilded, then turns into a Silver Age. Seneca's baroque
tragedies are as far removed from the neoclassic dramas envisaged
by Horace as Lucan's epic is from Virgil's—or Persius' satire from
Horace's. Yet the principle of continuity for which Horace fought
is more than classicistic: like order itself, it embraces not just Classical or Neoclassical art, but Baroque and Romantic within its
compass. Had Horace lived on, he might well have appreciated
Silver Latin poetry, seeing in it the same continuity through
change that his own work showed in relation to Lucilius and the
neoterics. He would surely have been pleased—and pleased, as
ever, with others' work because he was first contented with his own.

There is, indeed, a note of contentment in Epistles II, 1, that
is lacking in the *Ars*, although the two have much in common. In
both, Horace is the spokesman for order and right growth: the
artistic order perceived in literature, by which the writer proves
himself responsive to the moral order in nature, and the civilized
and civilizing order in the state. In both, too, Horace's personal
life and feelings are kept in the background, as though in their moment of fullest fruition they were wholly caught up in the larger
and more abiding literary and social order. The critical epistles

are thus a variation in the satiric key of ideas expressed in the beautiful autumnal lyrics of Odes IV. Yet Epistles II, 1 differs from the *Ars* in mood as well as subject matter. In the *Ars*, creation struggles to offset destruction, as in Lucretius' universe, but in II, 1, Horace seems to pause, to reflect on the accomplishments of his age. Much good has been done, may it continue! If he were alive, to hear his age spoken of as the Golden Age of Latin literature, he would undoubtedly smile, with a certain wistful irony, to be sure, but also in unembarrassed pleasure.

CHAPTER 8

The Persistence of Horace[1]

I T is quite impossible to give an adequate survey here of the development, extent, and vicissitudes of Horace's reputation and influence (not to add, the actual transmission of his poetry).[2] Let me therefore confine myself to indicating with what degree of success a few representative writers have revived some aspects of Horace's achievement.

I Renewal of Horatian Satire

Let us begin with satire, observing first that as Horace, by departing from Lucilius' spirit, made Lucilian verse satire into a stable and permanent form, so Persius and Juvenal gave strength and continuity to Horatian verse satire precisely by departing so clearly from the Horatian tone and intention. It is ironic but appropriate that in neoclassical satire, in England and France, his influence can scarcely be distinguished from theirs.

The satirist who most nearly approximates the "Horatian mode" is Alexander Pope; for as Horace stood on Lucilius' shoulders, Pope improved on Dryden, retaining his vitality but refining his wit (the following couplet belongs to "An Imitation of Horace, Epistles II, 1"):

> Late, very late, correctness grew our care,
> when the tir'd nation breath'd from civil war.

Pope's attempt to revive a truly Augustan style of "correctness" (typically, a Latinate word) in English life and manners is impressive. Not only does Twit'nam replace the Sabine farm, and Pope's relation to Bolingbroke imitate Horace's relation to Maecenas (itself, we remember, an imitation of Lucilius); but since Pope's neoclassical taste is at once moral and esthetic, it is fully embodied, like Horace's, in the polite, conversational form of verse satire, as in Epistles IV ("Of the Use of Riches"):

> You shew us, Rome was glorious, not profuse,
> and pompous buildings once were things of Use.
> Yet shall, my Lord, your just, your noble rules
> Fill half the land with Imitating-Fools; . . .
>
> In plenty starving, tantalized in state,
> And complaisantly helped to all I hate,
> Treated, caressed, and tired, I take my leave,
> Sick of his civil Pride from Morn to Eve;
> I curse such lavish cost, and little skill,
> And swear no Day was ever past so ill.

Pope is no "Imitating-Fool." He restores, not the externals of Horace's thought (though note the allusions to Satires II, 6 and II, 8), but the flexibility of the satiric verse form from which that thought is inseparable, the various and subtle modulations of diction, imagery, and rhythm that give Horace's satires their real excellence.

Yet in the last analysis, Pope stands with Juvenal, not Horace. Reading his works chronologically, we feel his growing awareness of sin and disorder in the world. Perhaps the order that Pope defends in his *Essay on Man* was too rationalistic and limited; perhaps, too, his Augustan aspirations, being less deeply rooted than Horace's, could not survive the political and economic realities of eighteenth-century England. In his reaction to what (in the Tory view) seemed the triumph of pride, corruption, and sheer dullness under the Hanoverians, he completes the satiric cycle, reverting to the *indignatio*, mock-heroic sarcasm, and grand invective of Juvenal and Dryden. The paradox is that in the "Epistle to a Lady" and "Dunciad IV," Pope's satire seems to reach its proper *telos*, so that we feel that Horace would have written like this had he "been brought down into the age"[3] of Nero, or Domitian, or (again, by the Tory view) George II.

But other forms than verse satire may convey the spirit of Horace's writings. Such a claim is often made for the *Essais* of Michel de Montaigne, although the studied undress or looseness, the rapid and eccentric shifts in subject matter, the undigested use of classical authors like Seneca and Plutarch—all this is exactly the kind of negligence that Horace criticized in Lucilius. And it shows the same self-confidence, magnanimity, and aristocratic pride. More Horatian, certainly, is Montaigne's attempt to "know himself," his flexibility, humor, and tolerance, and his insistence on contentment and tranquility as primary ethical goals. Horatian, too, is the development of his thought from a superficial Stoicism to the maturity of that beautiful essay, "De L'Expérience":

> Ce sont plaintes ingrates et iniques. J'accepte de bon coeur, et recognoissant, ce que nature a faict pour moy, et m'en agrée et m'en loue.

> (Such complaints are ungrateful and unfair. But I accept with all my heart and I appreciate what nature has done for me; I am content, and I give praise for it.)

We could be reading Epistles II, 2. Here is another man who has aged like good wine and "numbers birthdays gratefully." Yet our final impression of the *Essais* is of a baroque diffusion of form and thought, rambling, discursive, "satirical" in the old style, and reflecting an essentially unphilosophical and disordered life. If the prejudice is that of the eighteenth century against the sixteenth, it is nonetheless Horatian.

If we wish, therefore, to recover the pure wine of Horace's *Epistles*—the perfect mastery of style and of human conduct—we must return to eighteenth-century England, to Samuel Johnson's essays in *The Rambler,* which he began, appropriately, at the age of forty-two; for Johnson comes closest to Horace in combining the often incompatible qualities, of alert sympathy and serious moral judgment, that the best criticism of men or letters requires.

Thus it is evident that the generalizations toward which Johnson constantly is drawn, and which, like those of Horace, are too often removed from their vital contexts, arise from and are continually freshened by Johnson's sense of the "treachery of the human heart"—the snares in which men entangle themselves, and their constant failure to attain real and lasting satisfactions. This awareness, and the keen sympathy accompanying it, can be seen both in condensed observations—for example, that men grow weary of uniformity, that they are mainly preoccupied with small matters, or that "day and night, labour and rest, hurry and retirement, endear each other"—but also in entire essays, like that on Cowley (*Rambler 6*) from which the above quotation was taken, and which should be compared with Horace's Epistles I, 11, to Bullatius. Resting as it does on self-awareness, Johnson's charity toward human weakness shows perception, not just compassion. Thus biography is edifying because "We are all prompted by the same fallacies, all animated by hope, obstructed by danger, entangled by desire, and seduced by pleasure"; and that man is soonest condemned who "has so little knowledge of human nature" that (like Damasippus) he too quickly condemns others for their habits or occupations.

When Johnson says, "We are all prompted . . . ," the first person plural, like Horace's, is not simply didactic; for if Johnson's own openness to experience and empathetic grasp of human nature helps him to benefit others, his teaching is also self-teaching, part of a lifelong personal struggle to impose order on experience, to procure happiness, and to be wise and good. Indeed, like Horace, he constantly satirizes the man he was, or might have been: the "speculatist" who observes others but improves neither himself nor them, or the declaiming moralist who must himself be censured. Just as Horace moved away from diatribe, Johnson shows himself, in Mrs. Thrale's words, "averse to general satire"; and his aim is, not to "extinguish" the passions of men, but to redirect them into healthy and productive channels.

This does not mean that Johnson never writes ordinary "satire." There is the vignette of poor, sophisticated Euphelia, so bored in the country (*Rambler 42*), or the witty exposé of country "innocence and wisdom" in *Rambler 46*. There is also a fine self-irony, as when an essay begins, "MR. RAMBLER, you have often endeavoured to impress upon your readers . . . ." Clearly, the author knows his own limitations and keeps his didacticism within bounds. But a larger, more truly Horatian humor results from Johnson's successful but unending struggle to keep psychological awareness from turning to cynicism or despair. Even more than Montaigne's, his laughter is greathearted, a triumphant affirmation that, despite all obstacles, a man *can* be pleased, can grasp life and enjoy it. It is this laughter that warms our hearts after lesser wit has faded.

II *Renewal of Horatian Lyric*

Turning to lyric poetry, let me advance a paradox. Not one of the generally cited imitators of Horace ever did him justice, though all have their moments—Ben Jonson, Herrick, and Collins in England, Ronsard in France, Foscolo and Leopardi in Italy. Perhaps the failure of Andrew Marvell is typical. His love poems, like "To His Coy Mistress" and "The Garden," are Horatian enough, artful in rhythm and structure, in the "weaving" (still a favorite metaphor) of imagery and metaphor, and in the way Marvell uses inherited patterns of Metaphysical wit, as Horace used Hellenistic ones, to express ambivalent feelings about the power of time and the clash of ideal and reality. While his greater political odes, however, show a continuity of image and metaphor with those on love and religion, and some of the same inner conflicts have been pointed out in them, Marvell shows a more than Horatian uneasiness about his public role. Hence the increasing hollowness as he turns, significantly reversing Horace's direction, from lyric to satire.

To rediscover the Horatian spirit, we must look afar: not to writers like Marvell or Milton (although the latter's sonnets, composed during his years of political involvement while the epic waited, come closest to the Roman Odes in tone and attitude[4]) but to an early German Romantic, Hölderlin. The resemblance between Hölderlin and Horace is not of temperament, nor immediately obvious. While some of the German odes, like *An Die Parzen* or *Abendphantasie,* end on an Horatian note of contentment or resignation, Hölderlin more often feels driven irrevocably by yearning of heart or natural compulsion beyond the bounds of comfort and security,

der Heimat / Verehrte sichre Grenzen,

and out "to the deep," *in die Tiefe;* and as his visionary exaltation goes far beyond that of Horace, even in Odes I, 34 and III, 25, so do the loneliness and the despair that he feels at the incommunicability of his vision, or worse, its evanescence. Yet his strong passion is joined, like that of Keats (or Horace), with a remarkable quietness and simplicity of form, which ripens "to beauty's stillness," *zur Stille der Schönheit.*

Thus, in the Alcaic poem *Mein Eigentum,* Hölderlin seems not only to have mastered the Roman lyric form, but to have carried to a natural conclusion one of Horace's deepest meditations on nature and death.

> In seiner Fülle ruhet der Herbsttag nun,
> Geläutert ist die Traub und der Hain ist rot
> Vom Obst, wenn schon der holden Blüten
>   Manche der Erde zum Danke fielen.
>
> Und rings im Felde, wo ich den Pfad hinaus
> Den stillen wandle, ist den Zufriedenen
> Ihr Gut gereift und viel der frohen
>   Mühe gewähret der Reichtum ihnen....

> (The fall day rests in its fullness. Grapes are
> matured and hedges red with fruit, and many lovely
> blossoms have fallen to earth, to thank her; and in
> the fields, as I wander my quiet way, contented men
> find a ripeness of fortune making them rich in
> happy labor. . . .)

It could be Horace who goes on to pray for a resting place of spirit, a poetic inner garden "to cultivate with love's diligence always": only, as Horace felt drawn, in Odes II, 16 or I, 34, beyond the more usual "bounds" of security, we feel that Hölderlin is being drawn still further, against his will, into a realm where no serenity is possible and where neither Apollo nor the very light of human reason can save him. Contentment in the fullest Horatian sense is beautiful, but some men must be exiled from it, to wander like rootless spirits over the earth; and even art itself cannot provide a permanent resting place for the uprooted soul. The ode therefore heralds the ultimate disaster of Hölderlin's life, when, like his hero Empedocles, the dreamer and prophet who plunged into the volcano, the poet's sanity will be extinguished in formless, sightless passion. This is precisely the fate that Horace prophesied for the rebel turned madman—and avoided himself in his art and in his life. And yet there is no poetry in which (though fused with Pindar, Lucretius, and Catullus) the spirit of Horace seems more alive than that of Hölderlin.

In the end, therefore, we must be surprised: and not just at the vitality of Horace's poetry, his power to renew himself in modern satire and lyric, in the various and splendid creations of Pope or Montaigne, Johnson or Hölderlin. Rather, we return with new surprise to Horace's own unique and personal synthesis of thought and passion, which not only engenders so many literary children, but becomes inescapably part of the growth of every thoughtful reader. It is not just that we learn from Horace to enjoy moments of leisure, to take refuge from the complexities of the modern world on whatever Sabine farms are still available to us: but more, that this very enjoyment of leisure inevitably brings us back to the world of history—of air pollution, discrimination, poverty, and warfare. It is a harsh and confused world, and we would often prefer to escape from it. The classics themselves, Horace included, can be such an escape. And yet, is it not true that when Horace brings us, like Tyndaris and Maecenas, to the perennial shade of the Sabine farm, then he most enables and compels us—our hearts rekindled by wine, love, and poetry—to begin again the endless work of reconstruction?

Notes and References

Chapter One

1. On the Horatian ode generally, most useful are S. Commager, *The Odes of Horace* (New Haven, 1962), E. Fraenkel, *Horace* (Oxford, 1957), and L. P. Wilkinson, *Horace and His Lyric Poetry* (Cambridge, Eng., 1951). Also R. Reitzenstein, "Horaz als Dichter," *Neue Jahrbücher für das Klassische Altertum*, XXV (1922), 24-41, and "Eine neue Auffassung der Horazischen Ode," *NJA*, XXVII (1924), 232-41 (answering R. Heinze); F. Klingner, "Gedanken über Horaz," *Die Antike*, V (1929), 23-44, "Horazische und moderne Lyrik," *Die Antike*, VI (1930), 65-84, and "Horaz," *Die Antike*, XII (1936), 65-83; J. H. Waszink, "Zur Odendichtung des Horaz," *Gymnasium*, LXVI (1959), 193-204; and V. Pöschl, "Horaz," Fondation Hardt: *Entretiens sur L'Antiquité Classique*, II (Geneva, 1956), 93-115 (with a fine discussion, 116-27).

2. *Epistles*, II, 2, 124.

3. W. J. Bate, *The Achievement of Samuel Johnson* (New York, 1955), p. 66: "The term 'novelty', as Johnson uses it, suggests the whole seductive vista of everything we desire, do not actually need, and do not have at the moment."

4. For a different interpretation, see M. O. Lee, "Horace, *Odes* I, 38: Thirst for Life," *American Journal of Philology*, LXXXVI (1965), 278-81.

5. Mies van der Rohe.

6. Pyrrha, in *Odes*, I, 5.

7. Commager, *op. cit.*, p. 280.

8. Cf. M. H. Wheelock, *What is Poetry?* (New York, 1963), pp. 27-28 and 30.

9. Reitzenstein, "Eine Neue Auffassung," (*supra*, n. 1), p. 240.

10. Klingner, "Gedanken," (*supra*, n. 1), p. 39.

11. Cf. A. W. Verrall, *Studies Literary and Historical in the Odes of Horace* (London, 1884), pp. 34-36.

12. Commager, *op. cit.*, pp. 117-18; see also A. Y. Campbell, *Horace: A New Interpretation* (London, 1924), p. 110.

13. I must disagree here with the valuable remarks of W. Wili, *Horaz und die Augusteische Kultur* (Basel, 1948), pp. 243-44, and W. Ludwig, "Die Anordnung des vierten Horazischen Odenbuches," *Museum Helveticum,* XVIII (1961), 3.

14. *Epistles* II, 2, 58-60.

Chapter Two

1. On Horace's Satires and Epodes, there is much fine scholarship in Fraenkel, *op. cit.;* his earlier article, "Das Reifen der Horazischen Satire," *Festschr. R. Reitzenstein* (Leipzig, 1931), 119-36, is still important. On the beginnings of Roman satire, see now C. A. Van Rooy, *Studies in Classical Satire and Related Literary Theory* (Leiden, 1965). On Horace's relation to the Greek diatribe and Lucilius, there is much useful material in the commentary of Plessis-Lejay (Paris, 1916) and in G. C. Fiske, *Lucilius and Horace* (Madison, Wis., 1920); but Lucilius' work is better interpreted by M. Puelma Piwonka, *Lucilius und Kallimachos* (Frankfurt, 1949).

Good critical essays on Horace's satire generally are: U. Knoche, "Betrachtungen über Horazens Kunst der Satirischen Gesprächsführung," *Philologus,* XC (1935), 372-90, 469-82; R. A. Brower, *Alexander Pope* (Oxford, 1959), pp. 163-87; W. S. Anderson, "Imagery in the Satires of Horace and Juvenal," *American Journal of Philology,* LXXXI (1960), 225-60, and "The Roman Socrates: Horace and his Satires," in *Critical Essays on Roman Literature: Satire,* ed. by J. P. Sullivan (London, 1963), pp. 1-37. Also, on *Satires* I, 4: G. L. Hendrickson, *Amer. Journ. of Philol.,* XXI (1900), 121-42, and N. Rudd, *Amer. Journ. of Philol.,* LXXVI (1955), 165-75; on *Satires* I, 6: F. Klingner, *Philologus,* XC (1935), 305-14, and Rudd, *The Phoenix,* XV (1961), 196-212; on *Satires* I, 9: Anderson, *Amer. Journ. of Philol.,* LXXVII (1956), 148-66, and Rudd, *Phoenix,* XV (1961), 79-92.

2. *Satires* I, 114-19.

3. For the context, see Chapter 6. *Audacia* refers to the rashness of youth, who rush in, unaware (cf. *audet, Epistles* II, 1, 166) of how hard genuine poetry writing is, like other worthwhile things. Horace's early expectations, temper (*iratus*), and insecurity are contrasted with his present quietness, contentment (*praesidium regale* suggests Maecenas), and mature disillusionment with ambition.

4. *Epistles* I, 19, 23-25.

5. Catalepton XIVa, in *Appendix Vergiliana* (Oxford, 1966).

6. The same holds true for the pleasant erotic epodes, 11, 14, and 15, whose dominant spirit is one of ironic detachment.

Notes and References

7. *Ars Poetica* 79 (*lit:* "*his* special weapon"), but Horace's point is that the meter suits the mood.

8. The term, *malta,* means "effeminate"; early commentators identify "Maltinus" with the luxurious, effeminate, and casual Maecenas.

9. *Lucr.* II, 1-2.

10. See Puelma Piwonka (*supra,* note 1), p. 243, on Callimachus' ironic and personal use of the fable, and his doubt (p. 185) that Ennius' lark fable was more than an allegorical popularization of Greek thought.

11. Cf. Reckford, "Horace and Maecenas," *Trans. Amer. Philol. Assn.,* XC (1959), 195-208.

12. Cf. the *Schadenfreude* of *Satires* II, 8, where Horace's friends snigger at the maladroit host behind his back.

13. The phrase is Klingner's (*Die Antike,* XII, 69).

14. W. Y. Sellar, *The Roman Poets of the Augustan Age: Horace and the Elegiac Poets* (reprinted, New York, 1965), p. 44.

15. *Ars Poetica,* 438-44.

16. See N. W. DeWitt, *Classical Philology,* XXX (1935), 312-19, and A. K. Michels, *Classical Philology,* XXXIX (1944), 173-77. Philodemus' treatise "On Free Speech" can be read (with difficulty) in A. Olivieri's Teubner edition (Leipzig, 1914).

17. See, besides Puelma Piwonka (*supra,* note 1), the interesting remarks of Campbell, *op. cit.,* p. 53.

18. See Fraenkel, *op. cit.,* pp. 150-53.

19. The *auctor* is not Ennius, which would be confusing, but an undefined general figure; cf. N. Rudd, *Phoenix,* XIV (1960), 40-42.

20. Cf. *Epistles* I, 19, 14; *repraesentare* means to recreate the spirit of an earlier man, not just copy his mannerisms. See Campbell, *op. cit.,* pp. 283 ff.

21. See Anderson, "The Roman Socrates" (*supra,* note 1), 18-20.

22. *Lit:* "having been praised by Caesar." On the *lex,* see also *Epistles* II, 1, 150-55.

23. R. C. Elliott, *The Power of Satire* (Princeton, 1960), esp. Chapters 1 and 2.

24. C. Williams, *Witchcraft* (New York: Meridian Books, 1959), p. 71; also p. 72: "In fact, the authorities seem rather to have taken the view that to believe anyone could do it, to believe that one could oneself do it, and to do it were three degrees of preoccupation with the same evil."

25. *Homo Ludens* (London, 1950).

26. *Satires* II, 3, 11-12. This group of "fellow travelers" (*comites*) to the Sabine farm symbolizes the range and variety of the comedy Horace enjoys and uses.

HORACE

27. The following interpretation of Virgil's *otium* owes much to
F. Klingner's essays on Virgil in *Römische Geisteswelt* (Munich,
1961), and to V. Pöschl, *Die Hirtendichtung Virgils* (Heidelberg,
1964).

28. See Brower (*supra*, note 1), p. 173, on Horace's humorous
undercutting of the pastoral.

29. See Wili, *Horaz* (Basle, 1948), pp. 129 and 136.

30. See, generally, E. Wistrand, *Horace's Ninth Epode and Its
Historical Background* (Gothenburg, 1958); the poem may, however,
have been written some time after the battle.

31. Letter on Joyce (1949), cited by C. L. Barber in F. O. Mat-
thiessen, *The Achievement of T. S. Eliot* (New York: A Galaxy Book,
1959), p. 198.

Chapter Three

1. On Horace's relation to Greek models, see G. Pasquali, *Orazio
Lirico* (Florence, 1920), and Fraenkel, *op. cit.;* also Wili, *op. cit.,*
pp. 117-31; R. Reitzenstein, "Horaz und die hellenistische Lyrik,"
repr. in *Aufsätze zu Horaz* (Darmstadt, 1963), pp. 1-22; and, esp.
for the *recusatio,* W. Wimmel, *Kallimachos in Rom* (Wiesbaden,
1960). Also, on individual odes: J. P. Elder, "Horace *Carmen* 1.7,"
Classical Philology, XLVIII (1953), 1-8; Reckford, "Horace, Odes 1,
34," *Studies in Philology,* LXIII (1966), 499-532; V. Pöschl, "Dichtung
und Dionysische Verzauberung in der Horazode 3, 25," *Misc. A.
Rostagni* (Turin, 1963), pp. 615-25.

2. For Horace's metrical innovations, see L. P. Wilkinson, *Golden
Latin Artistry* (Cambridge, Eng., 1963), pp. 102-18.

3. See Reitzenstein, *op. cit.,* pp. 15-16.

4. Cited by Wilkinson, *op. cit.,* p. 113.

5. Quoted by R. A. Brower, *The Poetry of Robert Frost* (New
York, 1963), p. 6.

6. Pasquali, *op. cit.,* p. 466; see also pp. 363-65, 391.

7. Klingner, "Gedanken," *op. cit.* (*supra,* ch. 1. n. 1), 44; but see
V. Pöschl's qualifying remarks in *Fond. Hardt* (*op. cit., supra,* ch. 1,
n. 1), 106-08.

8. See B. Otis, *Virgil: A Study in Civilized Poetry* (Oxford, 1963),
pp. 5-40.

9. Wimmel, *op. cit.,* p. 11.

10. Compare also *Satires* II, 2, 103-5.

11. Freud's motto, ironically, was taken from Virgil: *flectere si
nequeo superos, Acheronta movebo.*

Notes and References

12. See A. Oltramare, "Horace et la Religion de Virgile," *Revue des Études Latines,* XIII (1935), 296-310.
13. See M. E. Taylor, "Horace: Laudator Temporis Acti?" *Amer. Journ. of Philol.,* LXXXIII (1962), 23-43.
14. *Prelude,* I, 357-400.
15. By a grammatical ambiguity, either the god or his follower may wear the vine-leaf crown of immortality.
16. But see S. Commager, "The Function of Wine in Horace's Odes," *Trans. Amer. Philol. Assn.,* LXXXVIII (1957), 68-80, esp. 79-80.
17. Contrast now *Odes* I, 6, 11.
18. See M. C. J. Putnam, *The Poetry of the Aeneid* (Cambridge, Mass., 1965), pp. 145-47.
19. Fraenkel, *op. cit.,* pp. 173-76.
20. Though untranslatable, the syntactical ambiguity is not undesirable, as Fraenkel argues (*ibid.,* pp. 171-72), but intentional (compare *Odes* IV, 2, 29-32) and deeply significant.

Chapter Four

1. The best general study of Horace's political poetry is V. Pöschl, *Horaz und die Politik* (Heidelberg, 1963); much of value, too, in Commager, *op. cit.;* Fraenkel, *op. cit.;* Pasquali, *op. cit.;* Wilkinson, *op. cit.;* Wili, *op. cit.* Also: K. Büchner, *Horaz* (Wiesbaden, 1962), pp. 125-38; G. Duckworth, "Animae Dimidium Meae: Two Poets of Rome," *Trans. Amer. Philol. Assn.,* LXXXVII (1957), 299-306; R. Heinze, *Vom Geist des Römertums* (Darmstadt, 3rd ed., reprinted 1960), pp. 190-204; H. Oppermann, "Zum Aufbau der Römeroden," *Gymnasium,* LXVI (1959), 204-17. For the historical background, see V. Gardthausen, *Augustus und seine Zeit,* I, 1-3 (Leipzig, 1891-1904), and R. Syme, *The Roman Revolution* (Oxford, 1939); also M. Hammond, "The Sincerity of Augustus," *Harvard Stud. in Class. Philol.,* LXIX (1965), 139-62.

See also, on individual odes: F. Solmsen, "Horace's First Roman Ode," *Amer. Journ. of Philol.,* LXVIII (1947), 337-52; V. Pöschl, "Die Einheit der ersten Römerode," *Harvard Stud. in Class. Philol.,* LXIII (1958), 333-46; W. J. Oates, *The Influence of Simonides of Ceos upon Horace* (Princeton, 1932), pp. 1-55; R. Hornsby, "Horace on Art and Politics (Odes 3.4)," *Classical Journal,* LVIII (1962-63), 97-104; B. Fenik, "Horace's First and Sixth Roman Odes and the Second Georgic," *Hermes,* XC (1962), 72-96.
2. In our *Vita Horati,* presumably going back to Suetonius, who had access to the imperial archives.
3. Fraenkel, *op. cit.,* p. 239.

4. Wilkinson, *op. cit.* pp. 64-65; A. La Penna, *Orazio e l'Ideologia del Principato* (Turin, 1963), pp. 13-27 (a very thoughtful critique.)

5. U. von Wilamowitz-Moellendorff, *Sappho und Simonides* (Berlin, 1913), p. 310.

6. See Cicero, *Pro Marcello,* esp. 8, 23-24, which looks forward in spirit and phraseology to Horace's demands. (Professor T. R. S. Broughton kindly referred me to this speech and discussed Caesar's failure with me.)

7. See M. Rostovtzeff, *Social and Economic History of the Roman Empire* (Oxford, 1926), pp. 38-74, esp. p. 74 and Plates.

8. See esp. Fraenkel, *op. cit.,* pp. 273 ff.

9. Hornsby, *op. cit.,* p. 99.

10. According to the *Vita Donati,* in *Vitae Vergilianae Antiquae,* ed. C. Hardie (Oxford: 2nd ed., 1957), pp. 27-28, Virgil and Maecenas read the *Georgics* to Augustus (for four days without stopping) when he was recuperating at Atella from the victory of Actium.

11. H. L. Tracy, "Thought-Sequence in the Ode," *The Phoenix,* V (1951), 116; better, Commager, *op. cit.,* p. 110: "The framework of daily routine provides a context in which the heroic becomes meaningful."

12. The interpretation of Campbell, *op. cit.,* p. 226, may be more suitable: "This last epithet is conventional, as if it were effortless; not pointed, because what is desired is not point but quietness."

13. M. E. Taylor, *op. cit., supra* (ch. 3, n. 13), p. 34.

14. N. Frye, *The Educated Imagination* (Bloomington, Ind., 1964), p. 140.

Chapter Five

1. Although my interpretations are independent of his, I refer the reader to Commager's excellent discussion (*op. cit.,* pp. 141-59, 235-91) of the poems on love, nature, and death.

2. On Lucretius' view of death, the complexity of which I could not examine here, see the commentary by C. Bailey, II (Oxford, 1947), pp. 994-96; W. S. Anderson, "Discontinuity in Lucretian Symbolism," *Amer. Journ. of Philol.,* XCI (1960), 4, 20, 23-24; C. Martha, *Le Poëme de Lucrèce* (Paris, 1896), pp. 133 ff., 142-46; A. K. Michels, "Death and Two Poets," *Trans. Amer. Philol. Assn.,* LXXXVI (1955), 160-70; and O. Regenbogen, "Lucrez," *Kleine Schriften* (Munich, 1961), pp. 347-50, 382.

3. *The Courage to Be* (New Haven: Yale Paperbound, 1959), pp. 70-78.

4. Martha, *op. cit.,* p. 212: "un sentiment sans illusion et sans orages."

Notes and References

5. See P. DeLacy, "Process and Value: An Epicurean Dilemma," *Trans. Amer. Philol. Assn.*, LXXXVIII (1957), 114-26, esp. 117-18.

6. Cicero, *Ad Fam*, IV, 5.

7. But the cow searching for her calf in Lucr. II, 360 is *desiderio perfixa*.

8. *Aeneid* X, 745-46, and XII, 309-10 (but perhaps borrowing from Horace):

olli dura quies oculos et ferreus urget
somnus, in aeternam clauduntur lumina noctem.

9. The English spelling, *V*irgil, loses the word play, *Veritas | Vergili;* also perhaps *ergo | Vergili* (but *virga*).

10. *Sent. Vat,* XIV.

11. Lucr. III, 931 ff. (a passage that greatly influenced Horace).

12. Lucr. III, 912 ff.

13. But see Commager, "Function of Wine," *op. cit., supra* (ch. 3, n. 16), p. 75, n. 15: "The overtones of natural decay [in the horticultural metaphor] add weight to the injunction."

14. Literally, "trusting as little as possible in the next one".

15. At least one schoolmaster got the point: see Dr. G. Richter, *Vier Schulreden* (Jena, 1897), pp. 12-18.

16. Cf. R. E. Grimm, "Horace's CARPE DIEM," *Classical Journal*, LVIII (1962-63), 313-18; also R. G. M. Nisbet, in *Critical Essays on Roman Literature: Elegy and Lyric*, ed. J. P. Sullivan (London, 1962), pp. 191-92.

17. Lucr. II, 29-33.

18. Cf. J. P. Elder, "Tibullus," in *Critical Essays (op. cit., supra,* n. 16), pp. 65-105.

19. Terence, *Eunuchus*, 56-63.

20. The ms. tradition is divided between *petet* and *petit*.

21. See Commager, *op. cit.*, pp. 322-24.

Chapter Six

1. On the philosophical epistles, C. Becker, *Das Spätwerk des Horaz* (Göttingen, 1963), is excellent. Also useful are E. Courbaud, *Horace: Sa Vie et Sa Pensée à l'Époque des Epîtres* (Paris, 1914); Fraenkel, *op. cit.;* J. Perret, *Horace* (Paris, 1959); Wili, *op. cit.;* and E. P. Morris, "The Form of the Epistle in Horace," *Yale Classical Studies,* II (1931), 81-114.

2. W. J. Bate, *The Achievement of Samuel Johnson* (New York, 1955), p. 78.

3. *Ibid.,* p. 74.

4. See the interesting remarks of Perret, *op. cit.*, p. 116.

5. R. Waltz, "Remarques sur l'Epître à Bullatius," *Revue des Études Latines,* XIII (1935), 311-21, argues that Horace develops Bullatius' pleasure in far-off places in his own way, then recalls both himself and B. to the larger wisdom of "return."

6. Cf. Reckford, "Horace and Maecenas," *Trans. Amer. Philol. Assn.,* XC (1959), 204-6.

7. Quoted by E. Drew, *The Literature of Gossip* (New York, 1964), p. 85; and cf. p. 87: "She ended in cheerful disillusionment and acceptance of all human limitations."

8. See Bate, *op. cit.*, p. 52.

Chapter Seven

1. On Odes IV generally, see Becker, *op. cit.;* Fraenkel, *op. cit.;* Wili, *op. cit.;* D. Norberg, "Le quatrième livre des Odes d'Horace," *Emerita,* XX (1952), 95-107; and W. Ludwig, "Die Anordnung," *op. cit., supra* (ch. 1, n. 13).

On *Epistles* II, 1 and 3, see Becker, *op. cit.;* C. O. Brink, *Horace on Poetry: Prolegomena to the Literary Epistles* (Cambridge, Eng., 1963); Fraenkel, *op. cit.* (on *Epistles* II, 1 only), and F. Klingner, *Studien* (Zurich, 1964), pp. 352-432.

2. R. W. Emerson, "Old Age."

3. Theocritus, XXX (Gow); see Pasquali, *op. cit.*, pp. 354 ff.

4. Robert Frost, from "Reluctance"; quoted by Commager, *op. cit.*, p. 291.

5. Fraenkel, *op. cit.*, p. 418.

6. See Becker, *op. cit.*, p. 162.

7. The question has been a troubled one: see Fraenkel, *op. cit.*, p. 418, n. 1.

8. On acrostics and word play in *Georgics* I, 424-37, and II, 315-42, see E. Brown, *Numeri Vergiliani* (Collection Latomus LXIII: Brussels, 1963), pp. 96-114, esp. 107 and 112 (on *ver*/ *Vergilius*).

9. See J. H. Finley, *Pindar and Aeschylus* (Cambridge, Mass., 1955), pp. 92-98.

10. Ludwig, *op. cit.*, pp. 8-9, makes the interesting suggestion that the political odes of Book IV are so placed as to pay tribute to Augustus for guaranteeing the private happiness of poetry writing and lovemaking.

11. Wili, *op. cit.*, p. 366, points out that after *Odes* I, 34, the poems, IV, 5 and IV, 15, are richest in indicatives.

12. E. Muir, *The Estate of Poetry* (Cambridge, Mass., 1962).

13. Klingner, *op. cit.*, p. 432.

Chapter Eight

1. For the interpretations in this chapter of Pope, Johnson, and Marvell, I am greatly indebted to R. A. Brower, *Alexander Pope* (Oxford, 1959), to W. J. Bate, *The Achievement of Samuel Johnson* (New York, 1955), and to L. W. Hyman, *Andrew Marvell* (New York: Grosset & Dunlap, 1964). For Montaigne I have used both the Pleiade edition, ed. by A. Thibaudet and M. Rat (Bruges, 1962), and *The Complete Works of Montaigne*, trans. by D. M. Frame (Stanford, 1948); and for Hölderlin, *Selected Verse*, ed. by M. Hamburger (Penguin Books, 1961).

2. Abundant material will be found in E. Stemplinger, *Das Fortleben der Horazischen Lyrik Seit der Renaissance* (Leipzig, 1906), and *Horaz im Urteil der Jahrhunderte* (Leipzig, 1921). For a succinct but inadequate survey in English, see G. Showerman, *Horace and His Influence* (Boston, 1922), and G. Highet, *The Classical Tradition* (New York and London, 1949), esp. chapters 6, 12, and 17.

3. Cf. Horace, *Satires* I, 10, 63 ff., on Lucilius!

4. See J. H. Finley, Jr., "Milton and Horace," *Harvard Studies in Classical Philology*, XLVIII (1937), 29-73.

Selected Bibliography

TEXT AND COMMENTARIES

WICKHAM, E. C., and H. W. GARROD, *Q. Horati Flacci Opera,* 2d ed., Oxford: The Clarendon Press, 1912. I have followed the readings of this text except at Odes II, 5, 16 *(petet)* and III, 4, 10 *(limina Pulliae).*

KIESSLING, A., and R. HEINZE, *Horaz.* I, *Oden und Epoden,* 9th ed., Berlin: Weidmann, 1958; II, *Satiren,* 7th ed., 1959; III, *Briefe,* 6th ed., 1959. The best commentary by far, full of information; E. Burck has added a long bibliographical appendix to each volume.

WICKHAM, E. C., *The Works of Horace.* I, *The Odes, Carmen Saeculare and Epodes,* 3d ed., Oxford: The Clarendon Press, 1896. II, *The Satires, Epistles, And De Arte Poetica,* 1891. The best commentary in English, especially useful on the dating of Horace's poems.

SECONDARY SOURCES

I *Books and Monographs (Those marked with an asterisk are of unusual importance.)*

* BECKER, C. *Das Spätwerk des Horaz.* Göttingen: Vandenhoeck und Ruprecht, 1963. An intelligent and thoughtful study of Odes IV and the Epistles. Argues convincingly that the *Ars Poetica* preceded Epistles II, 1.

*BRINK, C. O. *Horace on Poetry: Prolegomena to the Literary Epistles.* Cambridge: The University Press, 1963. A brilliant union of scholarship and critical interpretation, extremely useful to the student of the *Ars Poetica.*

CAMPBELL, A. Y. *Horace: A New Interpretation.* London: Methuen, 1924. A stimulating but very eccentric genre-centered approach to Horace's poetry.

COLLINGE, N. E. *The Structure of Horace's Odes.* London: Oxford University Press, 1961. Occasionally provocative studies in structural analysis.

* COMMAGER, S. *The Odes of Horace.* New Haven: Yale University Press, 1962. Witty, tactful, and often profound, C. introduces laggard Latinists to the "new criticism" at its best.

COURBAUD, E. *Horace: Sa Vie et Sa Pensée à l'Époque des Epîtres.* Paris: Hachette, 1914. A sensitive and charming book on the philosophical epistles.

FISKE, G. C. *Lucilius and Horace. University of Wisconsin Studies in Language and Literature,* VII. Madison, Wisconsin, 1920. Useful for Horace's use of diatribe material and borrowings from Lucilius, who, however, is much better understood by M. Puelma Piwonka, *Lucilius and Kallimachos* (Frankfurt, 1949).

* FRAENKEL, E. *Horace.* Oxford: The Clarendon Press, 1957. The best over-all study, combining much basic scholarship on Horace's life, writings, and sources with a profound sense of his personal development. A great book.

HOMMEL, H. *Horaz: Der Mensch und Das Werk.* Heidelberg: F. H. Kerle, 1950. Some good thoughts on the relation of Horace's political and philosophical ideas.

LA PENNA, A. *Orazio e l'Ideologia del Principato.* Turin: G. Einaudi, 1963. A stimulating socialist analysis of Horace's cooperation with the Augustan regime.

* PASQUALI, G. *Orazio Lirico.* Florence: Le Monnier, 1920; reprinted by photo-offset, 1964. An excellent and entertaining scholarly study, especially useful on the Hellenistic background of Horace's Odes.

PERRET, J. *Horace.* Paris: Hatier, 1959. Particularly good on the philosophical epistles. (A poor translation, by B. Humez [New York, 1964], exists in English.)

* PÖSCHL, V. *Horaz und die Politik.* Heidelberg: C. Winter, 1963. A short but profound discussion of Horace's political poetry.

SELLAR, W. Y. *The Roman Poets of the Augustan Age: Horace and the Elegiac Poets.* 1st ed., 1892; reprinted, New York: Biblo & Tannen, 1965. A sensible and witty book, still worth reading today.

WILI, W. *Horaz und die Augusteische Kultur.* Basel: B. Schwabe, 1948. An over-all view, particularly good on Horace's Ciceronian *humanitas* and the unity of his work.

* WILKINSON, L. P. *Horace and his Lyric Poetry.* Cambridge: The University Press, 1951. An extremely good introduction to Horace's Odes for the general reader, especially on questions of meter and translation.

Selected Bibliography

II   Related Works

Besides the books listed above (referred to in the Notes under the names of the authors), I have made considerable use of L. P. Wilkinson, *Golden Latin Artistry* (Cambridge: The University Press, 1963), and four excellent books on Virgil:

OTIS, B. *Virgil: A Study in Civilized Poetry.* Oxford: The Clarendon Press, 1963.
PÖSCHL, V. *Die Dichtkunst Virgils.* Vienna: Rohrer, 1950.
————. *Die Hirtendichtung Virgils.* Heidelberg: C. Winter, 1964.
PUTMAN, M. C. J. *The Poetry of the Aeneid.* Cambridge, Mass.: Harvard University Press, 1965.

I have also relied on G. Lugli, *Horace's Sabine Farm,* translated by G. Bagnani. Rome: L. Morpurgo, 1930. (That we can visit Horace's farm today is, however, a matter of faith, not reason alone.)

Good modern translations of Horace into English are:

The Odes of Horace, trans. by J. MICHIE, *The Library of Liberal Arts,* Indianapolis: Bobbs-Merrill, 1963.
The Satires and Epistles of Horace, trans. by SMITH PALMER BOVIE, *Phoenix Books,* Chicago: Univ. of Chicago Press, 1959.

III   Articles and Other Material

In the opening footnote to each chapter I have listed some articles (from thousands now existing) that seemed of unusual value. I would here only single out, as being equivalent in worth to any book listed above, the wise and beautiful essays on Virgil and Horace by F. Klingner which are now assembled, with others, in his *Römische Geisteswelt,* 4th ed. Munich: H. Ellermann, 1961.

General Index

Achilles, 23, 54, 55, 56, 133
Aeacus, 130, 131
Aeneas, 49, 57-58, 59, 62-63, 67, 69, 72, 76, 82, 89, 130, 133-4, 136-7, 143
Agamemnon, 131
Agrippa, 48-49, 68
Aithirne the Importunate, 37
Alcaeus, 15, 45-50, 65, 67-68, 71
Alexander the Great, 45
Anacreon, 104
Anchises, 133
Antony, 32, 45
Apollo, 48, 67-68, 79, 84, 132-3, 138, 151
Archilochus, 24, 38-39
Aristippus, 110, 115-6
Aristius Fuscus, 113, 115
Aristophanes, 25-26, 39
Aristotle, 25, 50, 116, 140-1
Atticus, 86
Augustus (Gaius Iulius Caesar Octavianus: also Octavian), 32, 35, 37, 42-43, 49, 53, 70-72, 74-82, 123-4, 132-3, 135-8, 141-4

Bacchus, 65-68, 95-96
Bellerophon, 126, 132
Bergson, 39
Bion of Borysthenes, 25, 34
Blake, 82
Bolingbroke, 28, 146
Burke, Edmund, 30

Caesar (1): see Julius Caesar
       (2): see Augustus
Callimachus, 24, 34, 45, 47-48, 59, 66, 104, 136
Cato the Elder, 45
Catullus, 14, 33, 42, 45-46, 76, 92, 98, 100-2, 125, 129, 151
Celsus, 107-8
Censorinus, 131
Chekhov, 123
Chesterfield, Lord, 28
Cicero, 35, 45, 50, 72, 86, 88
Cleopatra, 15, 46
Collins, 150
Coronis, 132
Cowley, 149
Cynics (and Cynicism), 24-25, 115
Cyrenaic School, 111, 115

Delia, 100
Dellius, 93-96
Diana, 132
Dickens, 119
Dido, 76
Diogenes the Cynic, 115
Domitian, 147
Donne, 92
Drusus, 123, 134-5
Dryden, 39, 146-7

Eliot, T. S., 43-44, 55, 123, 126
Emerson, 124
Empedocles, 151